Fun Times with Children

FunTimes with CHILDREN

Lou Heath and Rob Sanders

BROADMAN PRESS
Nashville, Tennessee

ISBN: 0-8054-3003-2
Dewey Decimal Classification: 790.1
Subject Heading: CHILDREN—RECREATION // CHURCH WORK
Library of Congress Catalog Card Number: 89-28126

Printed in the United States of America

Verses marked TLB are taken from *The Living Bible*. Copyright ©
Tyndale House Publishers. Wheaton, Illinois, 1971. Used by permission.

Verses marked GNB are from the *Good News Bible*, the Bible in
Today's English Version. Old Testament: Copyright © American
Bible Society 1976; New Testament: Copyright © American Bible
Society 1966, 1971, 1976. Used by permission.

Library of Congress Cataloging-in-Publication Data

Heath, Lou Mishler.
    Fun times with children / Lou Heath and Rob Sanders.
        p.   cm.
    ISBN 0-8054-3003-2 : $6.95
    1. Church work with children.   I. Sanders, Rob, 1958-
II. Title.
IN PROCESS (ONLINE)   89-28126
                                                           CIP

**To
All the Children
Who Have Taught Us to Have Fun Times**

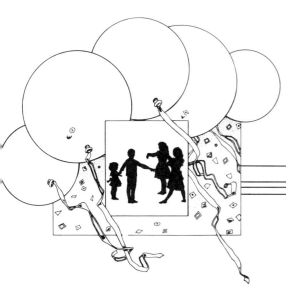

Preface

"The Valentine party for children and senior adults was a smashing success! The adults helped the children mix cookie dough, roll, and cut out Valentine cookies. While the cookies baked, the children made giant Valentine cards from poster board and ribbon scraps. The senior adults and children delivered the decorated cookies and Valentines to shut-ins. They loved it!"

Think about a party you remember.

What made it fun?

Who was there?

What games did you play?

What was the occasion for the party?

What did you eat?

How was the party room decorated?

If you can remember a party well enough to answer two or more of those questions, you had a fun time!

This is a book about fun times. Fun times for children. Extra special fun times for children! Fun times boys and girls will remember, and fun times you will remember. These fun times may even change the lives of children.

You will find that this is a book of ideas intended to help you create your own parties and fellowships. As you read, discover new and old ideas that you can make your own. Then begin planning fun times for children you know and love. Have fun!

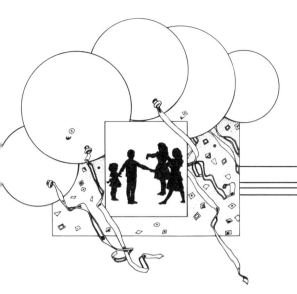

Contents

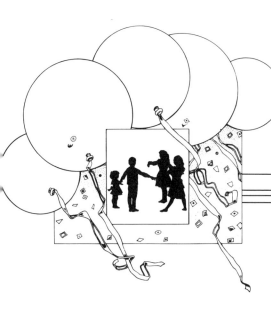

1
"Why Should I?"

Parties with a Purpose

"That was the most fun I've had in my whole life!"

"Oh, Mom, you should have seen the puppets! They were so funny!"

"We were in the summer book club so we get to have a Sundae Sunday!"

"Todd doesn't ever come to Sunday School. I know he had a good time at our Noah's Ark Party, though. Maybe he'll start coming now!"

"I'm glad there was *something* to do today."

Without knowing it, these children have something in common. They have all attended a party or fellowship that had a purpose. A purpose makes a party memorable. A party with a purpose indicates someone is interested in boys and girls and their enjoyment. A purpose changes a party into an event!

Determining a Purpose

Here are some general purposes that might lead you to plan a party, fellowship, or activity for children.

Just for fun.

To entertain.

To provide something to do during leisure time.

To make and enjoy friends.

In addition to these purposes, church-related fellowships may have other purposes. For instance:

To discover prospects.

To build self-esteem and encourage children.

To guide children to learn new skills.

To minister to other's, such as the senior adults or the handicapped,

To encourage church attendance.

To allow children to receive and give.

To help children know they are special.

To strengthen families.

To provide options for fun other than those offered in today's world.

☞ A Bible verse might also give us a purpose for a children's party or fellowship. For instance:

2 Timothy 3:15-17: "You remember that ever since you were a child, you have known the Holy Scriptures, which are able to give you the wisdom that leads to salvation through faith in Christ Jesus" (GNB).

Psalm 103:2: "Bless the Lord, O my soul, and forget not all his benefits."

Psalm 100:2: "Serve the Lord with gladness: come before his presence with singing."

Proverbs 3:5-6: "Trust in the Lord with all thine

heart; and lean not unto thine own understanding. In all thy ways acknowledge him, and he shall direct thy paths."

Matthew 28:19-20: "Go, then, to all peoples everywhere and make them my disciples: baptize them in the name of the Father, the Son, and the Holy Spirit, and teach them to obey everything I have commanded you. And I will be with you always, to the end of the age" (GNB).

1 Corinthians 3:9: "We are labourers together with God."

James 1:22: "Be ye doers of the word, and not hearers only." ✍

The purpose you choose for a party will determine everything else you do. Stop and think for a moment about an upcoming fellowship or party. Why have the party? What do you want to accomplish? What effect do you want the party to have on the lives of the boys and girls? A purpose will help answer these questions.

Stating the Purpose

Your party needs to have a written purpose.

Try writing the purpose in sentence form.

The purpose of our party is to . . . .

Keep writing and rewriting the purpose until you have a clear sentence. Be sure the purpose can be accomplished in the time allowed. Be careful, however, not to make the purpose so simple that it is accomplished too easily.

Here are a few party purposes gathered from some great party givers.

• To help children prepare to begin a new school year.

• To encourage fifth and sixth graders to share their Christmas joy with preschoolers at the inner-city day-care center.

• To discover prospects by asking children to invite nonchurch friends for a fun day in the sun.

• To thank children who have helped furloughing missionaries.

Can you see how a purpose will help as you plan a party? You can tell that the purpose will determine who you invite, what to wear, how to decorate, what games and activities to plan, and what refreshments to prepare. Make your party into an event—make it purposeful!

2
"What's It All About?"

The Theme's the Thing

A theme is to a party what a flower is to a butterfly. You just can't do without one! Like the purpose, the theme helps give direction to the other aspects of a party. If your theme is "Family Fiesta," invitations may be shaped as sombreros; decorations could include bright streamers and pinatas; tacos may be served from terra cotta pots; and children could play "Mexican Jumping Beans" and break a pinata filled with treats.

The theme of a party should not compromise the beliefs of your church or other work you do with preschoolers and children. Many churches are opposed to the secularization of Christmas. In those churches, having a "Santa Claus Is Coming to First, First" party is inappropriate. Likewise, themes with racial overtones would be offensive.

Don't let the theme dictate what you have to do. Don't let the theme overshadow the purpose. Choose a theme carefully and weave the theme and purpose together.

Themes can be placed in many categories. Here are some to get your mind humming!

Animal Themes

Cartoon Capers
"I Can't Bear It" Fellowship
Let's Go Zooing
Nature Expedition
Pig-Out Progressive Party

Bible Themes

Bible Families Fellowship
Bible Hero Party
Bible Olympics
Excavation Extravaganza
Festival of Booths
Good News Party
House-to-House Progressive Dinner
Noah's Ark Party
Promised Land Party
Sail with Paul Seminar
Share-a-Lunch with the Bunch
Shepherd and Sheep
Soup and Sing

Career Themes

Basic Training
Bright Idea Bash
Community Helper Holiday
Country Doin's Shindig
Hats! Hats! Hats!
"I Wanna Be" Party

Family Themes

Boy's Cookie Bake-Off
Family Circus Under the Big Top
Father-and-Son Hike
Father/Daughter Night
Mother/Daughter Chocolate
Not-Bored Games Tournament
Preschoolers and Parents Picnic

Holiday Themes

Jesus' Birthday Party
Christmas-Around-the-World Holiday Hunt
Exclusively Your's Valentine Party
"I'm a Patriot" Party
It's-Under-Wraps Christmas Party
Jesus' Birthday Party
Reason for the Season Party

International/Regional Themes

Around the World in Ninety Minutes
Brazilian Carnival
Family Fiesta
Far-Out, Far-East Party
Hawaiian Luau
Intercontinental Contests
Out-of-This-World Space Party
Tacos and Tunes
Western Roundup

Other Themes

ABC, 1-2-3
Apple Bash
Backward Party
Corn Dog Catastrophe
Cupcake Caper
Feminar
Follow the Clues: Find the Fun
Friendship Prescriptions
Girls Growing Gracefully Night
Good Ol' Days Party
Hobo Barbeque

Jelly Bean Jamboree
Mixed-up Daze
Night of Mysteries
No Girls Allowed—Boys Only
Paper Sack Party
Report and Rescue Rally
Say "Cheese" Party
Tacky Party
Tater Time
The Big Adventure
The Great Escape
Twinsy Party
Wanted Alive Jamboree
What Time Is It?

Reaching Out Themes

Adopt-a-Grandparent Valentine Party
Cereal Serial—Bring a Friend for Breakfast and
  Movies
Four Friends Follies
Good Samaritan Party
Shut-in Sing-along
Sundae Sunday
Tree Tea
You-Can-Help Fun and Canned Food Drive

Seasonal Themes

April Showers Bring May Flowers Party
Back-to-School Party
Bibles, Beach Balls, and Butterflies
Catch a Wave Party
Fall Family Fun Picnic
Free-at-Last Blast (School's Out)
Go-Fly-a-Kite Fellowship
Lunar Launch
Nature Expedition
Planting Party
Sand, Water, and Mud Day
Spring Fling/Winter Indoor Picnic
Star Search
Stuck on a Sticky Good Time
Summer Sip and Slide

Thanksgiving Open House
Winter Indoor Picnic

Special Interest Themes

Collections, Cookies, and Crazy Times
Color-Me-Happy Party
Craft Carnival
Everybody's Birthday Bazaar
Greatest Pet Show on Earth
Hobbies and Hamburgers
Mirror Reflections
Painting Party
Showing Off-Showing Art
T-Shirt Affair
There's Only One Me Party
Time Out for Tales
Wonderful Works Affair

Sports Themes

Bike Rodeo
Everybody Have a Ball
Game Shows and Good Times
Goofy Olympics

Hoops and Rings and Frisbee Flings
Jogging Jubilee
Play Off-Pay Off
Sink It, Swat It, Smack It
Tennis Shoes Tournament
Tyke Hike

Transportation Themes

Choo Choo Caper
No-Left-Turn Party
Ship Ahoy
Trucking into Summer
Up, Up, and Away

Themes are all around you. You may find inspirations on a billboard, in a grocery store, on television, from nature, or from the things children say. Some themes have longevity. Others may be associated with current fads. If children can identify with the theme, and the theme relates to your purpose without compromising your beliefs or those of your church, then go for it!

Make a list of your ideas for themes.

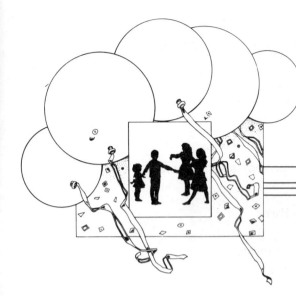

3
"Who's Gonna Be There?"

Deciding Who the Who Will Be

Who'll be at your party? Will your guests be four- and five-year-olds, third-grade boys, mothers and daughters, or all the elementary children in your church? After the purpose, the "who" of a party is the most important thing.

Think about children and how they develop and grow. Think about characteristics that will affect the activity you plan and lead. In general, children:

✓ respond to praise and postive comments.
✓ need simple, clear instructions.
✓ have short attention spans.
✓ want approval.
✓ need friends—children and adults.
✓ are easily excited.
✓ like to succeed.
✓ want to please.
✓ mimic adult behavior.
✓ need rules and guidelines.
✓ like variety and quick, short-term activities.
✓ like to be actively involved.
✓ are curious and inquisitive.
✓ are growing socially, mentally, physically, emotionally, and spiritually.
✓ enjoy fun!

Now think more specifically about children by meeting seven of our friends. We will begin with a two-year-old friend. (Parties for younger-than-two preschoolers are not so much for them as for adults giving the party.)

● Devin is two years old. She uses short sentences to communicate. Devin has taken control of her body and loves to walk, run, and jump. She is still self-centered but can relate to the feelings of others. Devin likes to play with others, but she likes to play alone too.

● Sam is a three-year-old friend. He is still self-centered. Sam may even snatch a toy from another child when he wants it. He can share too. Sam's moods vary. He is able to be a part of group activities and can sit for a while with a group. Sam is beginning to want to please adults.

● A four-year-old you should meet is Kara. She responds well to praise and demands less individual attention than younger preschoolers. Kara can play cooperatively and asks many questions. She can say more than she can understand. Kara works and learns well in a group.

● Jesse is five. Growing independence characterizes Jesse. He can play and work in a large group and with small groups of peers. Jesse has a vivid imagination and loves to pretend. He is in kindergarten and is developing many new skills.

He is developing large muscle control. He is very affectionate.

● Megan is ready to begin second grade. She likes to be active and is coordinated enough to use her small muscles to cut and draw. She can concentrate on one activity for six to seven minutes before needing a change of pace. She likes and needs rules, enjoys play-like games and make-believe, and doesn't mind being with girls or boys. She takes some responsibility for her own actions.

● Raymon is perpetual motion, quick-witted, and full of grins—a typical eight-, nine-, or ten-year-old child. He starts many activities and completes a few. He is interested in collecting anything, likes fair play, likes boys best. Raymon thinks for himself (but thinks concretely) and tells tall tales occasionally. He is friendly and likes to work with groups but is happy working alone. He doesn't like to lose and notices inconsistencies in adults.

● Tabitha is eleven going on sixteen! She is more interested in boys than they are in her. She does have close girl friends. Her physical and mental abilities have grown considerably the last few years. Tabitha can recognize and appreciate individual differences. She questions adults and needs reasons for obeying. She wants to help make rules and will sometimes go along with her peers even if it means breaking a rule. Although easily influenced by peers, she wants adult approval (though she may never let on).

■ Remember, sixth graders are *different!* They are not children, they are not teenagers. They want sophistication, but still enjoy childish pleasures. They sometimes like fellowshipping with only peers. Sixth graders *can* be grouped with younger children, especially if given some specific responsibility during the fellowship. ■

Guiding Behavior

Guiding children's behavior will keep you and the children happy. Children need to know what is expected of them. Simple, clear instructions will help. The following considerations will also help guide children's behavior.

Try out everything before you do it.

Keep everyone involved.

If something is a flop—then stop! And go to your next activity.

Children are more important than a game or an activity.

Don't expect children to act like adults.

Always have a back-up plan!

Stop while you're still having fun!

It is often helpful to establish rules or guidelines for children's behavior. Make the guidelines positive, avoid "no's" and "do not's." Here are some suggested guidelines:

Be kind.	Be helpful.
Cooperate.	Be polite.
Obey.	Listen.
Take turns.	Share.
Learn.	Be fair.

Print your guidelines on a poster, display them in the party area and call attention to them early in the party.

Determining Who to Invite

Your age and size does not determine your ability to have fun. Children may be grouped in a variety of ways for parties and fellowships.

The purpose of the party may help you determine how you will group children and who you will invite to the party. For instance:

PURPOSE: To strengthen father/son relationships

THEME: Pinewood Derby Day

FOCAL GROUP: fourth- through sixth-grade boys and their fathers (or other special adult males)

The season, event, or tradition itself may indicate who should be invited.

PURPOSE: To celebrate Jesus' birth.

THEME: Jesus' birthday party.

FOCAL GROUP: Two-year-olds through sixth graders.

The theme you choose may indicate who you will invite.

PURPOSE: To share what has been learned at Vacation Bible School with the families of children.

THEME: Family Beach Party

FOCAL GROUP: Families of preschoolers and children enrolled at Vacation Bible School.

Possible Fellowship Groupings

- Children and families
- Children and senior adults
- One age or grade
- Preschoolers and children (older children helping)
- All preschoolers and children (divided into age groups)
- Mother* (or father) and daughter
- Father* (or mother) and son
- Girls only (boys only)

Make your own list of ideas for grouping children.

(*Note: Or other special adult!)

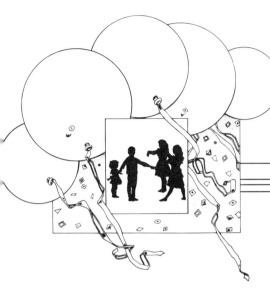

4
"When Is It?"

Scheduling a Good Time for a Good Time

When will you have the party? What day? What time of day? How long will the party last? The scheduling of a party will influence attendance, children's ability to participate and have fun, and the availability of adults to help.

How Do I Pick a Time?

When picking a time for a party, you need to:
Talk to children.
Determine what you wish to accomplish.
Check the church calendar.
Check public and private school calendars.
Informally survey a few parents and children's workers as to the feasibility of the date and time.
Consider the age and abilities of the children.

A party should have its own special time without competing with other events. Of course, Sunday School and other teaching times should not be used for parties. Here is a list of other times to avoid when scheduling the activity.
School nights
Church services
Family holiday times
Busy, hectic times
Sundays

Times when several children are involved in another activity, such as baseball
Vacation Bible School times
Revival times

You might sometimes schedule a party during a time that otherwise would be considered a "bad" time. For instance, when children are out of school for a teacher workday, during the Christmas holidays so parents can go shopping, or during a snowed-out day from school.

When Is a Good Time?

A party's theme may help determine a date and time for a party. Rain, heat, cold, or snow may be factors to consider when making fellowship plans. Seasons and holidays will help determine your schedule also. The following list of seasons and holidays may inspire your thinking about when to have a party.

New Year's Day   Winter
Martin Luther King Day   President's Day
Ground Hog Day   Valentine's Day
Saint Patrick's Day   Spring
April Fool's Day   Easter
May Day   Mother's Day
Flag Day   Summer

Fourth of July
Friendship Day
Grandparent's Day
Rosh Hashanah
Autumn
United Nations Day
Thanksgiving
Winter

Father's Day
Labor Day
Citizenship Day
Yom Kippur
Columbus Day
Fall
Hanukkah
Christmas

What Day?

During the school year Friday nights or Saturdays are the best days for fellowships. Days the children are out of school are also possibilities.

During the summer consider, weekdays, weeknights, or Saturdays.

What Time?

Here are the best times for parties for various ages of preschoolers and children:

Age	Time								
	8	9	10	11	Noon	1	2	3	4
2s-3s			x	x	x				x
4s-5s		x	x	x	x	x			x
6s-7s		x	x	x	x	x	x	x	x
8s-10s	x	x	x	x	x	x	x	x	x
11s-12s	x	x	x	x	x	x	x	x	x

Enlisting Party Workers

"Two can accomplish more than twice as much as one, for the results can be much better" (Ecclesiastes 4:9, TLB).

Yes, you *will* need help as you plan, prepare, and lead children to have fun times! Consider these sources when enlisting help: preschool and children's committees, Sunday School teachers, parents, senior adults, singles, older teenagers. Keep these party-giver/party-participant ratios in mind:

2s-3s	1 giver to 5 participants
4s-5s	1 giver to 6 participants
6s-7s	1 giver to 7 participants
8s-10s	1 giver to 8 participants
11s-12s	1 giver to 10 participants

"Commit your work to the Lord, then it will succeed" (Proverbs 16:3, TLB).

If it is important to plan fun times for children, it is important to pray for God's guidance as you plan. Pray before, during, and after a fellowship that boys and girls will have fun, that the fellowship purpose will be reached, and that lives of children will be changed for the good.

"We should make plans—counting on God to direct us" (Proverbs 16:9, TLB).

Plan with those who will be working with you. Evenly distribute the workload of the preparation and party schedule. Give people responsibilities that will use their abilities and strengths. Make planning fun and enjoyable—almost a party in itself!

The following verses from *The Living Bible* show qualities that are important as in working with and leading children:

"A wise teacher makes learning a joy" (Proverbs 15:2).

"A pleasant teacher is the best" (Proverbs 16:21).

"Show respect for everyone" (1 Peter 2:17).

"Try to live in peace even if you must run after it to catch and hold it!" (1 Peter 3:11b).

"If you wait for perfect conditions you will never get anything done" (Ecclesiastes 11:4).

Age	Time							
	5	6	7	8	9	10	11	Mid-night
2s-3s	x							
4s-5s	x	x						
6s-7s	x	x	x					
8s-10s	x	x	x	x	x			
11s-12s	x	x	x	x	x	x	x	x

How Long?

The length of the party should vary according to the age of the preschoolers and children.

Suggested Time Limits

2s-3s	Up to 1½ hours
4s-5s	Up to 3 hours
6s-7s	Up to 4 hours
8s-10s	Up to 5 hours
11s-12s	Up to 5 hours (and lock-ins and over-nighters)

What Is the Schedule?

Here is a suggested way to use the time planned for a party:

- 20% Get acquainted, beginning activity, name tags
- 50% Games, activities, crafts, stories, devotion.
- 15% Refreshments
- 15% Closing activities

Any Other Suggestions?

Here are a few additional tips on scheduling times and dates for parties:

✔ Not too early.
✔ Not too late.
✔ Quit while you're still having fun.
✔ Overplan (have more to do than time to do it).
✔ Always keep in mind the age of the child.
✔ Plan no more than 15-20 minutes for simple refreshments (20-30 minutes if a meal is served).
✔ The younger the child, the shorter the party.

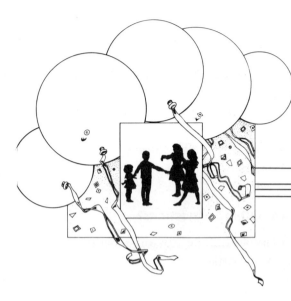

5
"Who, Me?"

Invite Them and Delight Them

Publicity is the attention getter and the information giver for parties and fellowships. Publicity in its simplest form gives answers to five questions:

Who?
What?
Where?
When?
Why?

Your publicity for a party may include phone calls, visits, mailouts, displays, bulletin boards, posters, handouts, announcements, newsletters or newspaper articles, and, of course, invitations.

Basic Publicity Guidelines

1. *Begin early, but not too early*. Beginning to share information three weeks before a party should give you plenty of time. Invitations should be mailed ten to fourteen days prior to a party and reminders to children may be made from the time of the mailing to the day of the party.

Start your publicity with a teaser (a little information) and build on it as the weeks progress.

2. *Use a variety of methods to share information*. The more you repeat your message and the more ways you find to repeat it (poster, flyer, invitation) the more children and parents will remember.

3. *Use color*. Notice the colors and patterns children are wearing. This will clue you into combinations that will excite children *now!* The current fad might be mixing a variety of bright colors, or wearing checkerboard or Hawaiian patterns.

4. *Be specific in your message*. The message should be simple enough for children to understand, yet give parents all the information they need.

5. *Make it look good*. Don't clutter your publicity. Keep it simple. Remember, however, that simple does not mean plain!

6. *Be different*. Be funny. Use words that demand attention, or make a combination of elements that is unusual. Being creative does not necessarily mean being artistic. Being creative means being different!

7. *Think like a child*. Ask: What will be appealing, interesting, and exciting to children in *my church* today? Remember, too, that children can help with publicity. They can draw a logo, letter a handout, make a bulletin board, or design invitations.

8. *Use a logo and establish colors for each party or fellowship*. A logo is a drawing (your's or some-

thing cut from another source) that is associated with a certain event or happening. Using the logo and designated colors again and again will help children and parents recognize the publicity and associate it with the event.

9. *Where to go for help with publicity.* Consider these sources for help in publicizing a party or fellowship:
- Preschool and children's teachers
- Parents
- Artists and architects in your church
- Talented teenagers
- Staff
- Children
- Public relations committee of your church

Invitations

The invitation is the primary publicity tool for a party—and the most personal.

Designing an invitation before doing other publicity work for a party may help you accomplish your task more easily. Invitations may be purchased. Making your own invitations allows for more creativity, however. Invitations may be copied or printed if a large number needs to be made.

From *A* to *Z,* here are invitation ideas. Some descriptions are given. Use the basic idea and let your imagination go to work!

A

ADVENT WINDOW. As windows are opened, information about the party is revealed.

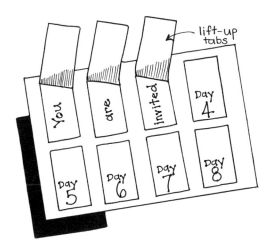

AIRLINE BOARDING PASS. Use with "Up, Up, and Away" party.

ALPHABET MACARONI. Glue macaroni to form all or some words of the invitation.

B

BAG. Use for invitation for "Paper Sack Party." Label the bag, "A Fun Time Is in the Bag."

BALLOONS. Inflate and write a message with a permanent marker. Deflate and mail.

BASKET. Deliver invitations in small baskets or hang on door.

BIRTHDAY CANDLE. Send along with invitation to an "Everybody's Birthday Bazaar."

BUTTONS. Use on paper clothing-shaped invitations.

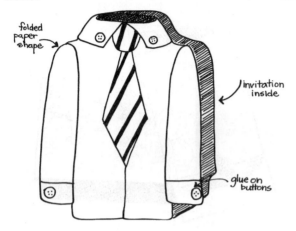

BUTTERFLIES. Enclose a sticker or picture with a "I Am Changing" invitation.

C

CALENDAR. Highlight the date as well as the information about your party.

CLOCKS. Information is written on the face of different kinds of clocks and watches.

CLOTH. Gingham and bandanas make good invitation covers.

CODES. Number, letter, and picture codes can be a novel way for children to get information about a party.

COMICS. Write your own message in the balloons above the characters' heads.

CONFETTI. Enclose in an invitation for an extra surprise.

COTTON BALLS. Add texture to clouds and lambs.

CRAYONS. Send a crayon with an invitation to a "Color Me Happy Party."

CROSSWORD PUZZLE. Clues and puzzle words tell about the party.

CUPCAKE LINERS. Party information is written on the liner for a "Cupcake Caper" party.

D

DIPLOMA. A diploma can invite sixth graders to a graduation party.

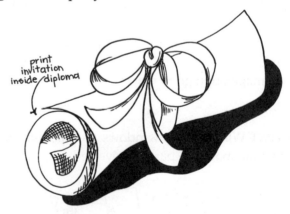

DOLL CHAIN. Cut out paper doll chains and print party information on them.

E

EGGS. Put an invitation inside a plastic egg and deliver it.

ENVELOPES. Print information on graduated sizes of envelopes. Place envelopes inside each other.

F

FILMSTRIP PIECES. Cut filmstrip and attach to invitation to the "Cereal Serial" party.

FLAGS. Send small American flags with an invitation to a patriotic party.

FLOWER PETALS. Write information on paper petals or include dried petals with an invitation.

FOLDED. Fold invitation into a triangle, accordion fold, or fanfold.

FORTUNE COOKIE. Place your own message in the cookie before delivering to children.

FLOWER SEED PACKETS. Send with an invitation to a "Spring Fling."

G

GIANT PEEP BOX. Prepare party information and place inside a giant peep box. Display at child's eye-level in a highly visible place.

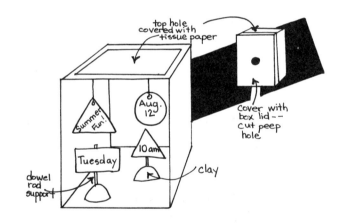

GIRAFFES. Send a giraffe to be colored by preschoolers for a "Let's Go Zooing" party.

GLUE ON SEEDS. Glue seeds to form a party message.

GUM. Send a stick of gum with the message; "We're stuck on a doggone good time!"

H

HAND-DELIVERED COOKIES. Deliver cookies with party invitations.

HOT SAUCE PACKET. Enclose with a "Family Fiesta" invitation.

I

ICE-CREAM SPOON. Print invitation on wooden ice-cream spoon for a "Sundae Sunday."

INGREDIENTS. Invite children to bring ingredients for party refreshments.

INVISIBLE. Write party invitation with white crayon on white paper. Send instructions for child to lightly color the invitation with pencil, water-based marker, or pastel crayon to reveal the hidden message!

J

JELLY BEANS. Hand out jelly beans as reminders about the "Jelly Bean Jamboree."

JOKES. Surround an invitation with jokes.

K

KITES. Make oversized kites from poster board. Some information can be printed on tailpieces.

KNOCK-KNOCK. Write invitation as a knock-knock joke.

> Knock-knock.
> Who's there?
> Wooden.

Wooden who?
Wouldn't you like to come to a party?

KEYS. Send a key with a "Trucking into Summer" invitation.

L

LABELS. Use labels from canned goods to invite children to a "Hobo Barbeque" or to bring canned goods for a needy family.

LEAF. Send fall leaves to invite children to the "Fall Family Fun Picnic."

LIFESAVERS. Use colored paper reinforcements to symbolize lifesavers and enclose a miniature package of Lifesavers with the invitation. Print "U R A Lifesaver" on the envelope.

LOLLIPOP PEOPLE. Print invitation on paper clothes and tape to the lollipop.

M

MAPS. Use maps to give directions to the party.

MAZES. Use to guide children to party location or to give party information.

MIRROR PAPER. On the outside of the invitation print: "Who is invited?" Glue mirror paper on the inside so child sees his reflection.

MIRROR WRITING. Write invitation backwords so the message can be read by holding it in front of a mirror.

MIXED LETTERS. Cut letters from newspapers and magazines to form a "ransom note" look.

MOVABLE PARTS. Make movable parts to the invitation that children will manipulate to find information about the party.

N

NEWSPAPER HEADLINES. Use photo copies from paper to make an "Extra! Extra! Read All About It" invitation.

NOTE IN BOTTLE. Place party invitation inside small plastic bottle.

NOTES. Illustrate a bowl of soup with musical notes to invite children to a "Soup and Sing."

O

OPEN UP. Invitation will have some part that will open to reveal information about party.

OUTLET. Draw an electrical outlet and plug. Use the saying, "Plug into a good time."

P

PACKAGE. Invitation is placed inside a small wrapped package.

PAPER CLIP. Send a colorful paper clip with an invitation. Ask children to attach the clip to their clothing for the party.

PAPER PLATE. Write the invitation around the plate so it has to be turned to be read.

POCKET. Glue a pocket shape onto paper. Insert invitation in pocket.

POEMS. Example: Poem for an outside mother/ daughter "Tree Tea."

> Of all the mothers in the world,
> You're the best one there could be.
> And we want to honor you,
> This Saturday with tea.
> So let's dress up and meet our friends,
> Under Mrs. Edward's tree.
> We'll visit and laugh, and have such fun,
> I know that you'll agree.
> So Mother, dear, won't you please say,
> That you will go with me?

POPSICLE STICK. Cut a hot dog bun shape from manila paper, making two slits at the bottom of the bun. Print the invitation on the stick and slide it through the slits to form a hot dog.

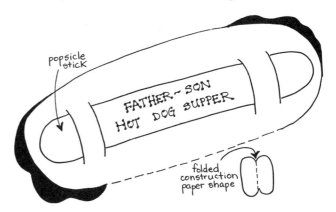

POP-UP. Make 3-D cards with an object that pops up when opened.

PRESCRIPTIONS AND PILL BOTTLES. Write an invitation as a prescription for a fun day. Enclose in pill bottles and deliver to children.

PRINTS. Make thumb, hand, and footprints on invitations to invite children to the "I Am Special Party."

PUZZLES. Mail or give out puzzle pieces that reveal information about party.

Q

QUESTION MARKS. Write the invitations as questions on question marks.

QUICK PULL. Print party information on pieces of construction paper. Glue to a ribbon. Insert in envelope so children can "pull out" the invitation.

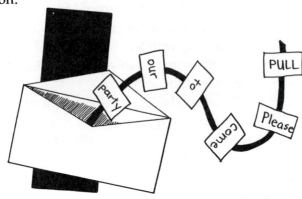

R

REBUS. Use pictures in place of words wherever possible on invitation.

RECIPE. On a recipe card, write an invitation that uses words such as: *add, mix, stir,* and so on.

RECORDED MESSAGE. Send a printed invitation asking children to call for a recorded message.

The message will give party information.

REPORT CARD. Grade your party before the party: Fun—A+. Refreshments—A+.

RHYMES. example:

Come to our party
At half past two,
Bring your best friend,
We'll have fun things to do!

RIBBON. Instruct children to tie ribbon around their wrist to remind them to come to a party.

RIDDLES. Example: What do you get when you add kites, ice cream, and games?

Answer: Fun at Saturday's "Go Fly a Kite Party!"

ROAD SIGNS. Print party information on stop, school crossing, or other road sign shapes.

S

SCROLLS. Make scroll invitations. Roll, tie, and deliver.

SEA SHELLS. Make a double shell. Glue a "pearl" in the center and mail to mothers and daughters for a "Feminar" invitation.

SHAPES. Consider using these shapes: doughnut, T-shirt, hats, truck, shell, apron, whale, swimsuit, book, egg, recording, sleeping bag, ball, blocks, umbrella, box.

SHOELACE. Tie a tennis shoe shape with a shoestring to invite children to a field day of fun.

SILHOUETTES. Use presidential silhouettes to invite children to a patriotic party.

SNOWFLAKES. Use paper doilies to invite children to a "Winter Indoor Picnic."

STORYBOOK. Use several pages and a cardboard cover to make a storybook invitation.

STRAWS. Send a straw along with a "Summer Sip and Slide" party invitation.

T

TEA BAG. Mail a tea bag in the invitation to a mother/daughter "Tree Tea."

TELEGRAM. For instance: "Saturday, November 3. STOP. 9:00 AM-12 noon. STOP. Come to 'Time Out for Tales.' STOP."

TEXTURED MATERIAL. Sandpaper, wood shavings, and wallpaper add variety to invitations.

THERMOMETER. Use a saying such as: "Winter's over and things are heating up. Come to our 'Sand, Water, and Mud Day' for a good time in the sun."

TOKEN AND TICKETS. Send tokens and tickets to be used as admission to a party or for games at a party.

TREASURE MAP. A treasure map will lead children to a treasure chest of fun.

U

UMBRELLA. Send party favor umbrellas along with invitations to "April Showers Bring May Flowers Party."

V

VALENTINE. Make red construction paper hearts and glue them to white or gold doilies.

VINES. Draw a growing vine with information written on leaves.

W

WESTERN POSTERS. Instant pictures of children mounted on an invitation saying: "You're wanted for a Western Roundup!"

WORD SEARCH. Information will be hidden in a word search puzzle. For example:

```
X Y Z F R I D A Y X Y Z
A P R I L F I F T H X Y
Z X Y Z S I X P M X Y Z
X Y Z A T C H U R C H X
Y D O N O T B E L A T E
```

WRAPPING PAPER. Wrapping paper can make colorful background for invitations.

WRITE AROUND A SHAPE. Lightly outline a shape on paper. Print party information around the shape. Erase the outline.

X

X RAY. Draw an "X ray" of a skeleton. Use it to invite to children to the "Excavation Extravaganza."

Y

YOURSELF. One of the best invitations is a personal visit.

Z

ZIPPER BAGS. Invitations can be unique when placed in a zipper sandwich bag with an item related to the party.

6
"What Are We Gonna Do?"

Fun Things for Fun Times

Puppets! Music! Field Trips! Games! Stories! Movies! Crafts! Is there any end to the possibilities? Absolutely not! The choices for party activities are endless.

The first consideration in choosing activities is the party's purpose. As you know, everything should relate to the purpose of the party. The second consideration is the theme of the party. The theme will help determine what kinds of activities to use, names of activities, and props to use.

To maximize fun, and minimize distress, remember the children who will be attending the party. Children come in all shapes and sizes and with a great variety of abilities. It is important that the self-esteem of each child be preserved by planning activities that will allow everyone to be successful.

When it comes to competition for children, your motto should be: "Low or no." Younger preschoolers should have no competitive activities. If competitive games are used with older preschoolers and children, they should be few and far between. When using competitive games, every effort should be made to help children have fun whether they are the winner or the loser. (Does the term, *loser* tell you why competitive games should be limited at church?)

Children + party + fun = controlled chaos.

If you plan to have complete control every minute of every fellowship, you might as well stop reading now! Seriously, children will be loud, boisterous, and outgoing when they are having a good time.

Our activity plan includes three parts:
• Getting things started;
• Keeping things going;
• Wrapping things up.

Getting things started includes: greeting each child as she arrives, making name tags, icebreaker activities, and get-acquainted activities.

Keeping things going is the main part of the party activity. It is a high-strung, involved time that includes games, field trips, mission action activities, and other activities you choose.

Wrapping things up is when the party begins to slow down and you start preparing the children for going home. This time might include devotions, reading or telling a story, prayer, and quiet games.

Here are some tried and proved ideas for getting things started, keeping things going, and wrapping things up.

Getting Things Started

Things to remember when greeting a child.

• Greet every child as he enters the room. (Stoop down and greet the child eye-to-eye!)

• Call each child by name. (Use those name tags!)

• Be natural and enthusiastic. (Don't fake it!)

• Immediately involve the child in an activity with someone he knows. (Make introductions, if you need to!)

• Quickly begin ice breakers and get-acquainted activities. (There's no time like the present!)

Ice Breakers

FIND YOUR MATCH, MATE. Prepare on 3 by 5 index cards, pairs of names. For instance, Adam-Eve, peanut butter-jelly, Mickey-Minnie, or pencil-paper. As children arrive, give each a different card and ask him to keep it a secret until everyone has a card. At the command, "Find Your Match, Mate," children will hunt for their matching partner. When matches are made the pair sit down together.

SAY "CHEESE." Use an instant camera to snap a picture of each child as he or she enters. Mix the photos and give each child a photo other than his own. The object is to meet the person whose picture you hold and find out the person's favorite way to eat cheese. (On pizza, cheeseburger, toasted, and so on.) Each child will introduce his "all-American" friend to the group.

THE GREAT TRADE-OFF. Prepare a large number of one-inch squares from five colors of construction paper. Mix all the squares together and then divide them into four piles. On one pile write the number "1" on each square. Number the other piles, "10," "13," and "22." Hide the squares throughout the party area. The object of the game is to find and collect squares you think are most valuable according to their color or number. Children can trade with one another in any combination. After five to ten minutes, call the children together. Give point values and have each child add up his points.

Point values may be . . .

Purple = +20	green = −5
gray = +5	pink = +10
orange = −10	ones = +10
tens = +5	thirteens = −20
twenty-twos = 0	

TICKTACKTOE, THREE FRIENDS IN A ROW. Middle and older children will enjoy this pencil and paper game. See the example.

HUMAN TICKTACKTOE, Before children arrive, make a giant ticktack toe gameboard on the floor with masking tape. (Remove as soon as the party is over!) When children arrive, randomly divide them into two teams. With masking tape, allow one team to make Xs on their shirts. The other team will make Os on their shirts. Each team will huddle and learn each other's names. (Allow three to five minutes.) Designate an area where each team will sit. An adult leader begins the game by pointing to one child on the X team. The child stands immediately. The X team members must shout the first and last name of the child in this manner: "Jon. Jon Meyers. Our friend, Jon Myers!" The team must then let Jon choose where he will stand on the ticktack toe gameboard, and applaud whatever choice he makes. (Failure to name the child, or to applaud his choice, results in a loss of the team's turn!) Play continues until a team has three in a row or all squares are full. Why not play this game several times?

FINGERPLAYS. Preschoolers will enjoy fingerplays and action songs. These activities help children relax. Good resources abound but you can make up your own fingerplays too.

PANCAKE PANDEMONIUM. Have the children get in a single file line, facing in one direction. (If there are more than ten children, form a second line.) Tell the members of the line they are pancake batter. The first person in the line begins the game by saying, "Pour it!" and squatting. Each person in turn says and does the same thing. When the last person has said "Pour it!" and squatted, he says, "Flip it!" and turns around, to face the opposite way, remaining in a squatted position. The phrase and action passes back up the line. When the last person has "flipped," he stands and shouts, "Gobble it!" Once again the line repeats, in turn, the phrase and action. If using more than one team, the teams may try to "out bake" each other.

DO YOU BUY THAT? Think of ten grocery items with which the children can associate a jingle or commercial saying. Line the items up in a single file line on the floor. Place a masking tape line on each side of the groceries (the lines should be about three feet from the items.) Divide the children into two even teams, Team A and Team B. Number the children on Team A from one to ten and the children on Team B from one to ten. Each team will sit behind a different masking tape line; ones facing each other, twos facing each other, and so forth.

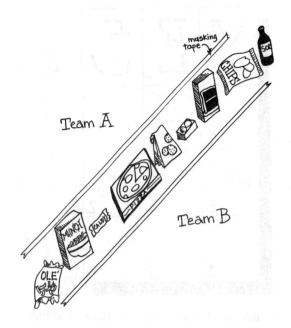

The leader begins the game by saying a part of a commercial jingle and calling out, "Number eights, do you buy that?" The two team members with the number eight race for the item. The first one reaching the item takes it back to his team. If the correct item was chosen, the team scores one hundred points. If the match is not correct, the item is placed back on the line. Continue saying jingles and calling numbers until products are all "bought."

Get-Acquainted Activities

SILENT BIRTHDAY HUNT. Children must be old enough to know their birthdate to play the game. The object of the game is for a child to find every person in the group who was born the same month he was. The difficult part of the game is that the hunt for birthday matches must be done in silence. Players may mouth the month or use hand signals. As the game begins to wind down, call time. Allow each group to share their names and birth months.

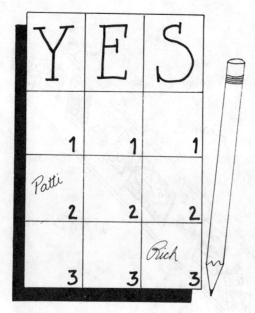

YES! Provide 5½ by 8½-inch cards (see illustration) and a pencil for each player. A child will fill each square with autographs from nine children. When cards are completed, an adult leader will call a space and a name of a friend. For example: E-2, Andra Bradley. The child with Andra's name in the E-2 square will draw a smiley face over the name. Play continues until all children are introduced or a child has three in a row (up, down, or diagonally.) When a child has three in a row, he shouts, "Yes!"

MY SECRET SELF. As children arrive, give them a 4 by 6 index card and a felt-tip marking pen. Ask them to write the name of someone they would like to be on a name tag (Superman, Donald Duck, George Washington, and so on.) Place the "make-believe" names in a hat or decorated box. Children may use a second card to make a name tag with their real name. Fasten name tags to clothing with rolled strips of masking tape.

Form a circle. Place the "make-believe" name tag container in the center of the circle. Ask a child to draw a "make-believe" name from the container and read it to the group. Children will raise their hands and guess which child placed

that name in the container. When a match is made, the child will tape the "make-believe" name tag on, also. Allow only three guesses before a child identifies himself.

PUZZLE PARTNERS. You will need one sheet of construction paper for each two children you expect to attend your party. Use various colors of paper. Cut each sheet into two puzzle pieces. Mix all the puzzle pieces together.

As children arrive, they will print their name on a puzzle piece and attach it to their clothing with masking tape. Each child needs to find his "puzzle partner." Partners will introduce each other to the rest of the group.

BEANS! I HAVE NEVER! As each child arrives, give him twenty beans in a plastic sandwich bag. Seat children in a circle with a bean pot in the center of the circle. The object of the game is to have the most beans at the end of the game. Players try to name things they have never done that they think others have done. If a person has done what the leader says, she must put one of her beans in the pot. For instance, a player may say, "I have never ridden a ten-speed bike." Every player who has ridden a ten-speed bike must put a bean in the pot. Let each player have at least one turn trying to stump the group.

Keeping Things Going

Inside Games

CHARIOT CHASES. This game needs to be played in a large room. Remove all tables, chairs, and other objects from the room. Mark off a rectangle on the floor with masking tape (at least four feet from every wall), forming an arena. Divide the children into chariot teams of six. Provide a sturdy beach towel or heavy blanket for each chariot team. Assign each chariot team a home base near the tape on the inside of the rectangle.

towel
or
blanket

Each chariot team member must sit on the end of the towel and be pulled around the outside of the rectangle by two team members. Speed is the name of the game as chariot teams race back to their home base. Every team member must ride once and pull twice. Caution riders to hold firmly the sides of the towel as they are pulled around the arena. All chariot teams are winners since everyone rides!

TWO BY TWO. Give each child a card with the name of an animal printed on it. Every animal name must be given to two children. Caution children to keep their animal name a secret. At a signal, each child will begin making the sound of her animal and will try to locate her animal match by the sound he is making. The "problem" is that everyone is making the sound of their animal too!

When the partner is found, the pair may sit down together. To make the game even more difficult, older children may play this game with lights out!

RELAYS. There is an endless variety of relays to play with children. Here are some favorites:

(1) Banana Relay. You will need two bananas. Divide the children into two equal teams. Place the teams in two single-file lines facing in the same direction. The object of the game is to pass the banana up and down the line quickly. Teams will first pass the banana down the line over their shoulders, then back up the line between their legs. When the banana gets back to the first player, he must peel it and eat it. The first team to pass, peel, and eat the banana is the winner.

(2) Stinky Shoe Relay. You probably remember this game from your childhood. Children place their shoes in a pile at the end of the room. (Leaders need to mix the shoes so pairs are separated.) Divide children into two teams. Line the teams up at the end of the room opposite the shoes. At a signal, the first child in each line will race to the "stinky shoe" pile, locate his shoes, put them on, run back to his team, and tag the next player. The first team with shoes on are the winners.

(3) You-Look-Ridiculous Relay. Provide two sets of large adult clothing: jeans, shirt, hat, shoes, gloves. Place each set of clothes in a suitcase at one end of the room. Divide the children and leaders into two teams and line the teams up at the end of the room opposite the suitcases. The first person in each line will run to the suitcase, put on all the clothes, pick up the suitcase, race

back to his line, take off the clothes, and put them back in the suitcase. The second player puts on all the clothes at the starting line, races with the suitcase to the opposite end, removes the clothes, puts them in the suitcase, and leaves it there before running back to his team and tagging the next player. Play continues until every team member has a chance to "look ridiculous."

PENCIL-AND-PAPER GAMES. Younger and older children enjoy activities that use brain power as well as hand power. Some ideas include:

(1) Mazes
(2) Crossword Puzzles
(3) Word Search
(4) Secret Codes
(5) Matching Games
(6) Fill in the Blanks
(7) Dot-to-Dot
(8) Acrostics
(9) Scrambled Words

SHAPE-UP. Provide a cassette tape player or record player and quiet music. Ask children to spread out throughout the room, facing a leader who stands at the front of the room. When the music begins, an adult can lead children in gentle fluid movements. After a few minutes, the adult may call on a child to lead the group in movement. Change leaders frequently.

BALLOON BALLYBALL. Make a square on the floor with masking tape. Inflate five large balloons. Have the children sit around the square, facing the center. The object of the game is to keep the balloon in the air by passing it in order to each person in the square.

Once the children have mastered passing one balloon, add a second and a third. If a player misses the balloon, or causes another player to miss the balloon, he turns his back to the center of the circle and plays from that position. This game fosters teamwork and cooperation, and players will soon learn to gently tap the balloon to the next player.

KID OVERBOARD. Supplies: a cassette tape player or record player, recording, and masking tape.

With masking tape, make a "ship deck" on the floor. Make the deck big enough for most of the children to stand inside. As the music plays, children march around the deck. When the music stops, children scramble to get on the deck and not be left "overboard!" Children may do anything necessary to get on board. They may stand on one foot, be held by another player, and so on.

If any children are not on board, the leader calls, "Kid overboard!" Children on board then try to "save" as many "overboarders" as possible without falling overboard themselves.

You can make the game harder for older children by moving the tape to make the deck smaller. Those who are unable to get on board can give advice and cheer those still in the game.

ADAPTING OTHER FAVORITE GAMES. Many television game shows and board games can be adapted for use at a children's party. You may change the name, add questions related to your theme, or make the game Bible related. Have fun being creative!

Outside Games

KRAZY KICKBALL. This is a wonderful outside game! You will need two plastic hoops for bases and a playground ball or kickball. Do *not* use a soccer ball!

Place the two hoops one hundred feet apart on a large playing field. One hoop will be home base, the other, first base. The only out-of-bounds area is the area behind home base.

Divide children into two teams. One team begins in the field, the other is at bat. The team in the field has a pitcher (who stands halfway between home and first base) and a catcher (who stands behind home base). The other players on the fielding team may stand any place on the field where they think the ball may come.

Each team will choose its kicking order. The order will be resumed where it ended. A kicker has only one ball rolled to him. A player is out when he misses the ball rolled to him, his fly kick is caught, he is forced out at first base, or he is tagged out (the ball may *not* be thrown at a player). Each team is allowed three outs each inning.

A player does not have to leave first base until he chooses to. Any number of players may be on first base at the same time, waiting for a chance to score. Runs are scored only when a player crosses home base.

THE GREAT ALPHABET ADVENTURE. Print the letters of the alphabet down one side of an 8½ by 11-inch sheet of paper. Provide copies of the sheet and pencils for each child at the party. Divide the children into pairs and give them their sheets and pencils.

The assignment: Go outside and find something that begins each letter of the alphabet. Print the name of what you find on the sheet (example: *A*-ant, *B*-butterfly, *C*-Christopher Thomas, and so on.) Some children will find very clever solutions to the assignment! Allow ten-fifteen minutes and then call the pairs together to share. (You might want to eat dry alphabet cereal as you share.)

MOONLIGHT VOLLEYBALL. Supplies: A dark night, a volleyball net, a volleyball painted with fluorescent paint (some toy stores have blow-up plastic balls with a place to insert a glow stick), and children! Make sure no outside lights are on to spoil the effect of moonlight volleyball. Divide into two teams and play as you would regular volleyball. You'll be surprised how difficult and fun the glowing ball makes this game!

SLIDE-AWAY. To prepare this activity, you will need fifteen to twenty feet of wide, heavy plastic (such as that used in landscaping), a rake, a large yard or field near a water outlet, a water hose, and children in swimsuits. Use the rake to clear the field of rocks, sticks, and other dangerous items. Spread the plastic on the grass and begin spraying the surface with water from the hose. (The moisture will help the plastic stick to the grass.)

Allow one child to slide at a time until they are accustomed to the surface. Continue spraying the plastic with water. Children may compete for furthest slide, most original slide, and in other ways they choose. If the area gets too muddy, pick up the slide and move to a new location!

SCAVENGER HUNTS. Children are collectors and, thus, are fans of scavenger hunts. The day has passed, however, when children can safely go to the homes of strangers to collect scavenger hunt items. Therefore, scavenger hunts should be held on the church property, at a park where you are having your party, or by going to the homes of church members. Children should always be accompanied by adults.

(1) Camera Scavenger Hunt. Each team of children will need an instant camera loaded with film, an adult sponsor with a car, and a set of assignment cards. Assignments may include: Photograph all group members in front of an American flag; photograph a bell, and so on.

Place each of the assignments (up to eight) in a sealed envelope. Give a set of assignments to each adult sponsor.

The teams will open the first assignment before leaving the church. Each of the following assignments may only be opened after the previous assignment is completed. The winner is the first team back with photos of the completed assignments. To extend the activity, ask each group to write a creative story, using the photos as their inspiration. Read the stories to the entire group for a wonderful ending to a super activity.

(2) Strung-Out Scavenger Hunt. The items children will gather on this hunt are normal scavenger hunt fare—toothpick, flyswatter, diaper, stick of gum, or anything else you can think of. Children will go to the home of church members with their list of items. (You may want to pre-arrange homes for them to visit, or let the visit be spontaneous.)

What makes this hunt different is that a long piece of yarn is strung through the belt loops of each child, tying the team together. (If a child does not have a belt, the string will be loosely tied around his waist.) As the children travel in the car, walk to and from houses, and return to church, they must remain tied together without breaking the string. The winning is the one which collects the most items on their list and remains strung together.

(3) Nature Scavenger Hunt. Divide children in either pairs or small groups. Set boundaries for the hunt. Give each group a list of things to collect: flower, small leaf, wood, something red, something alive, something that smells, and so on. It will help groups if they have a paper bag in which to place their collected items. Blow a whistle when time is up. When all groups have returned, each group can share their findings.

THE GLOB. This outdoor game is simple to play. Mark off a large playing field in a grassy area. One person is "The Glob." Everyone else tries to avoid "The Glob" by quickly walking within the boundaries. When "The Glob" tags a player, that player attaches himself to "The Glob" and together they go after more victims. Play continues until everyone is a part of "The Glob!"

REFRESHMENT TREASURE HUNT. This activity can be adapted to fit many party themes and refreshment choices. The following example is a Banana Split Treasure Hunt.

Gather the ingredients for banana splits. Look around the party area, whether inside or outside. Decide where the refreshment ingredients can be hidden. (For example: in a hollow tree, behind a flowering bush, in a cabinet, and so on.) Make clue card giving directions to each ingredient. (For instance, if the first ingredient is in a hollow tree: "Take eighteen giant steps. Turn around twice. Reach inside. Its bark is worse than its bite.") Before the activity, have an adult helper hide each ingredient along with the clue to another ingredient.

As children find each ingredient, they collect another clue. The process continues until all ingredients (except the ice cream) are collected.

The ice cream can be located by using a treasure map drawn on brown wrapping paper. Burn the edges of the paper to make the map look old. With ingredients in hand, the children follow the map to the ice cream and make their banana splits.

WATER GAMES AND ACTIVITIES. Who doesn't like getting wet in the hot summertime? Try these age-old favorites for a splashing good time!

(1) Water Balloon Fights. Divide the children into two teams. Mark off the boundaries each team must stay behind. Children will enjoy the preparation of the balloons as much as the fight itself. Each team will need 200-300 balloons and a water source. Allow ten to fifteen minutes for teams to prepare the "ammunition" by filling balloons with water. The fight begins when the first balloon is tossed and ends when the last splash is

made. For extra fun, invite the pastor, church staff, and Sunday School teachers to participate. (Squirt guns and wet sponges are fun, too, if high-powered guns are outlawed!)

(2) Water Painting. This is a special activity for preschoolers and younger children. Provide buckets of water, clean paint brushes in various sizes, paint rollers, and paint pans. Children may paint on sidewalks, buildings, and each other. One children's minister even let children "paint" his car with water! As soon as the water evaporates, a new "painting" can take its place.

(3) Make Your Own Bubbles. Mix one part liquid detergent and three parts water. You may need to add more detergent if bubbles are hard to form. Add a few drops of liquid vegetable oil and food coloring.

Try all kinds of bubble-blowing tools—commercial tools, loops made with chenille wire, drinking straw, several straws taped together with masking tape, plastic hair curlers, and so on.

If several children are blowing bubbles, consider making the solution in a large dishpan.

(4) Wet Tug-of-War. Older children will enjoy this wet fun! You will need a long, heavy rope, and a shallow wading pool filled with water. Divide the children and leaders into two teams; try to keep the teams even in terms of strength. The rope is stretched across the pool and each team grabs an end of the rope. Tug! Huff! Pull! Puff! The winner is the team that remains dry. Or is it the team that gets wet? If you don't want to use a wading pool, place a ground-soaker hose (the kind with many holes) between the two teams.

(5) Mud Play. A little dirt and a little water can make for lots of muddy good times. Guide children to make mud pies, mud castles, mud cities, and mud messes. Clean the children with a hose when you finish. Grubby clothes are considered proper attire for this activity.

OBSTACLE COURSE. You may make your obstacle course as elaborate or as simple as you wish. The age of the children will help you determine how complex the course should be. All sorts of items may be used. Here are some suggestions: large cardboard boxes, tires, ladders, cones, jump ropes, logs, boards, chairs, tricycles, sawhorses, and wading pools. Lay the course out on a large, grassy area. Mark the start and finish lines with a flag, sign, or crepe paper streamers. When setting up the course, always keep the safety of the children in mind!

Before children run the obstacle course, an adult needs to demonstrate how to complete the course. Use a stopwatch to clock the adult's time and allow the children to compete for better times. (This means children are not competing with each other, but with the adult!)

Field Trips

Here are enough field trip ideas to fill a van!

- Synagogue
- Theater
- Ball Game
- Museum
- Park
- Ice-Skating Rink
- Miniature Golfing
- Roller Skating
- Water Sliding
- Amusement Park

- Factory
- Zoo
- Historical Site
- State Park
- Nursing Home
- Publishing Company
- City Hall
- Fire Station

Field trip reminders:

(1) Prepare, distribute, and collect signed permission slips from each child's parents.

(2) Tell the parents how the children should dress.

(3) Make advance preparation by securing transportation, buying tickets, if necessary, planning the route to and from the destination, and letting parents know when you will return to the church.

(4) Before leaving, tell the children what you expect of them and any rules they will need to follow on the field trip.

Crafts

SIDEWALK CHALK. You will need several colors of dry tempera paint, plaster of paris, water, five-ounce paper cups, plastic spoons, and measuring spoons. Guide the children to measure two tablespoons of powdered tempera and three tablespoons plaster of paris into a paper cup. Mix the dry ingredients with a spoon. Measure in three tablespoons of cold water and stir for one minute. Allow the mixture to dry for one hour. Then children can peel off the paper cup and use the chalk to draw on the sidewalk. (Rain or a water hose will wash away the drawings.)

ONE-OF-A-KIND T-SHIRT. Each child will need a T-shirt. (White or pastel colors dye best.) You will also need rubber bands, two or three colors of powdered dye, a plastic bucket for each color of dye, a clean garbage can or other large container filled with cold water, hot water, rubber gloves (for adults), and a clothesline. Let older children string the rope between two trees. Prepare the dyes in the buckets.

To begin the project, guide children to "bunch-up" material in several places on the front, back, and sleeves of the T-shirt. Tightly place a rubber band around each "bunch." Teachers will dye the "bunches" in colors the children decide, or the whole T-shirt may be dipped in one or more dyes. Children will remove rubber bands, rinse their shirts in the cold water, and hang the shirts to dry. If you do not have a clothesline, hang the shirts on bushes or a tree.

STICKY BUMPER SIGNS. You will need light colored or patterned adhesive-backed paper, permanent felt-tip marking pens, various kinds of stickers, scissors, construction paper, and a Bible. Print several of your favorite Bible verses on construction paper. Guide the children to read the verses with you before beginning the activity.

Guide the children to cut the adhesive-backed paper into 4 by 9-inch rectangles. Permanent felt-tip markers may be used to letter a Bible verse on each rectangle. Decorate the "Sticky Bumper Signs" with stickers. Children may stick the signs on their bicycles or give them to parents and other adults for their cars. Encourage children not to put the "Sticky Bumper Sign" on a car without permission!

SEE-THROUGH MURALS. Here's a fun way to involve a lot of children in an activity and decorate the windows of your church, a nursing home, or fast-food restaurant at the same time. (Be sure to ask permission before painting!)

You will need: various colors of dry tempera paint, liquid dishwashing detergent, water, plastic jars with lids, paintbrushes in various sizes, spoons, newspapers, and paper towels.

Mix each color of paint in a separate plastic jar by mixing liquid dishwashing detergent into dry tempera. Add the detergent slowly and stir until it is of a thick, yet usable consistency. If the paint remains too thick, slowly add water, stirring until the paint is a bit thinner. Do not make the paint too thin or it will run when you paint the windows.

The children will use the paint and brushes to paint scenes on the inside of windows. Choose a theme for your paintings (such as Christmas, autumn, or the Fourth of July). Spread newspapers on the floor before beginning. Leave the paintings on the windows as long as you like. To remove, wipe the paint off with wet paper towels. (The detergent base of the paint will make this easy.)

MUSICAL BREEZE CHIMES. You will need a small clay flowerpot (with a hole in the bottom) for each child, jute or heavy string, masking tape, scissors, and six to ten jingle bells for each child.

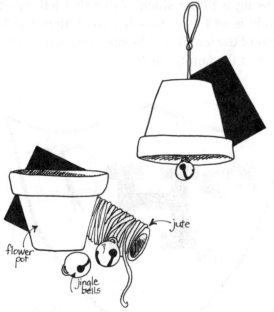

flower
pot

jingle
bells

jute

Cut a three-foot length of jute and tie a knot in one end. Thread the jute through the hole in the bottom of the flowerpot so the pot can be suspended upside down. Cut a piece of jute for each jingle bell. Jute pieces may be three to eight inches long (a variety of lengths are best). Tie each piece of jute to a jingle bell. Tape the opposite end of the jute inside the rim of the flowerpot. Hang the "Musical Breeze Chime" near an open window or on a porch.

RUBBED MEMORIES. Supplies: drawing paper, masking tape, crayons, pencils or charcoal, inter-esting surfaces. Possible things to rub: leaves, sidewalks, bricks, window screen, fabric, grasses and flowers, and many other raised or textured surfaces. Place drawing paper over the surface and tape down the corners. Small objects may be placed on a flat surface before taping the paper over them. Gently rub with a crayon, pencil, or piece of charcoal and watch a memory emerge!

FUN WITH DOUGH. There are many recipes for making dough that can be formed into figurines, Christmas ornaments, paperweights, and other gift items. Here is one recipe: 4 cups flour, 1 cup salt, $1/2$ cup water. Mix the ingredients together to a doughy consistency. Dough may be refrigerated in a covered container for several days. Warm to room temperature before using.

Children may shape the dough into the figures they desire. Working on aluminum foil makes cleanup easy. To attach dough pieces or to seal edges, dip fingers in water and rub the dough surfaces with wet fingers. If you are making an ornament, fashion a hook out of a paper clip and push it into the back of the ornament before baking.

Place the aluminum foil holding the shapes on a cookie sheet and bake in a 350° oven for one hour. After the shapes cool, they may be painted with tempera or acrylic paints.

ORIGINAL WRAP-UPS. Children enjoy making gifts for others as part of the fellowship activities. Making wrapping paper to cover a gift is another enjoyable activity. You will need newspapers, butcher paper, scissors, liquid tempera paint, shallow bowls, potatoes, cookie cutters, and butter knives.

Cover the floor around the work area with newspapers. Cut a three-foot section of paper for each child. Children may cut potatoes in half, press a cookie cutter into the flesh of the potato, and then use a butter knife to cut away the part of the potato that is not a part of the design. The process forms a stamp for printing.

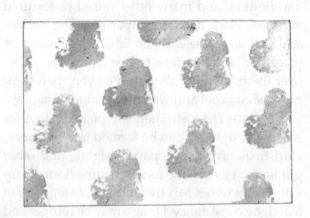

potatoe printer

Pour a little tempera paint in a shallow bowl. Children may dip their stamps in the paint and then press them on the paper to make designs. Children may make crazy designs, repeated designs, or use several colors of paint. The cookie cutters themselves may be dipped into the paint to make a design. A simple alternative to using paint is to allow children to use felt-tip markers and crayons to make scribble or other designs.

CRAYON CREATIONS. The following activities are based on the same art methods. The procedure calls for children to draw pictures on white, prewashed fabric with wax crayons. When drawings are completed, lay the drawing on a thick stack of newspapers, with the crayon side pointing up. Place a damp paper towel over the drawing. An adult then irons the paper towel until it is dry. This will cause the wax to be removed, yet leave the colored picture imprinted on the fabric.

(1) Creative Crayon Banner. Using the party theme or Bible verses, children can make banners. Give each child a three-foot long strip of fabric for his banner. The bottom of the banner may be cut into a point, scalloped, pinked with shears, or have an inverted triangle cut from it.

After the child has drawn his picture and you have ironed the banner, attach the top of the banner to a dowel rod with tape, staples, or thread. Hang the banner with yarn attached to the ends of the dowel rod.

(2) Creative Crayon Place Mats. Cut four rectangles, squares, or circles for each child. The children can illustrate the shapes with scenes that show happy family living. When completed, the shapes may be used for place mats at home. (Be prepared to provide enough place mats for children having more than four family members.)

(3) Creative Crayon Family Crest. A crest is a drawing within a shield shape that tells what a family is and what they believe. Often, the first letter of the family's last name is used at the focal point of the family crest.

cardboard shield covered with fabric

From an eighteen- by twelve-inch sheet of heavy cardboard, cut a shield shape for each child. Children may draw their family crest on a rectangle of fabric slightly larger than the cardboard. Suggest that they put the initial of their last name in the center of the drawing and then illustrate family members and favorite family activities. When the drawings have been completed and ironed, guide the children to attach them to the cardboard shields. Tape the excess fabric to the back of the shields.

Mission Activities

Serving and helping others can be a noble product of a children's party or fellowship. Choose from the following activities:
- Pot flowers and deliver them
- Rake yards   • Wash windows
- Bake and take cookies to prospects
- Make visits   • Write letters
- Make greeting cards
- Lead in a devotion time for others
- Clean churchyard   • Go caroling
- Deliver in-church mail

- Present a puppet drama
- Collect and deliver food baskets
- Give a party for an inner-city day-care, school for the blind, or children' home
- Wash cars for church staff
- Adopt a grandparent
- Have a used-clothing drive
- Carry firewood   • Shovel snow
- Gather and read mail to elderly

- Read the Bible or other reading material to a shut-in
- Water plants   • Carry packages

Wrapping Things Up

Devotions and Bible Study

The most appropriate way to conclude a party at church is to lead the children in a Bible study or Bible activity time. You will find many helpful resources for Bible study ideas, but here are a few of ours.
- Read a Bible story
- Read a Bible storybook
- Read a missionary story
- Read a book that emphasizes a Christian principle
- Have a praise time
- Pray together
- Sing songs
- Learn and say Bible verses
- Whisper a secret assignment to each child that encourages him to act out Christian principles (for instance: invite a friend to Sunday School).
- Watch a short movie or filmstrip that teaches values or good morals
- Invite a Christian community helper (firefighter, police officer, school teacher) to share how he or she lives for Jesus on his or her job
- Play recordings of appropriate music
- Invite pastor, minister of music, or children's minister to lead a devotion or give a testimony
- Ask a missionary to speak
- Use drama, role play, skits, or puppets
- Invite a musician to share her talents
- Lead a Bible drill or hymnal drill
- Lead a campfire service
- Use Bible games to review learning
- Have an "I Am Thankful for . . ." time
- Play musical instruments
- Write and read poems

Conclusion

Plan how to get things going, keep them going, and wrap them up. Plan more activities than you have time for and you will avoid the "what do we do next" syndrome. Have fun with the children you love!

Additional Activities
(List other activity ideas to use.)

7

"Did You See That?"

More Than Crepe Paper and Balloons

Decorations—the physical environment of a party—make the first impression to the party goer. Decorations can change a fellowship hall into a foreign country or a parking lot into Noah's ark!

You may choose to use decorations to give a surface statement about a theme, or decorations may be elaborately expanded to enhance a theme.

For small parties, less is best when it comes to decorations. Too many decorations may confuse younger children or be overly stimulating.

Children today are accustomed to colorful, attention-getting input. So, decorations may be quite elaborate. Allowing children to help plan and prepare decorations for a party may give you sound guidance in making your plans.

Decorations do not need to be expensive. They *do* need to be appealing and interesting to children.

Decorations for a party may include:
• name tags
• walls, ceiling, and doorway decorations
• table coverings and table runners
• centerpieces
• serving pieces
• focal areas

Decorations may be expanded outside the party area. Balloons tied to an outdoor church sign, banners of colorful fabric hanging from pillars, or a mannequin dressed in party-theme attire can set the tone for a party and communicate, "There's fun inside!"

You can also lead children to a party with decorations. Question marks on sidewalks or hallways can direct children to a mystery party. Bales of hay, forming a maze would be a fun way to lead children to a "Country Doin's Shindig." Flowerpots and garden tools placed outside a door will direct children to a "Spring Fling" fellowship. Footprints on the floor can encourage children to find their way to fun.

Look at the following ways to develop decorations around a theme.

Country Doin's Shindig

Outside: Clothesline with overalls, apron, and long johns hanging beside a washtub.
Name Tags: Farm animal shapes. Hang around necks with binder twine.
Walls, Ceilings, Doorways: Murals of farm life on walls. Hang quilts on the walls. Cover doorways with butcher paper and paint to resemble barn doors.

Table coverings: Gingham.
Centerpieces: Baskets of plastic eggs surrounded by toy farm animals.
Serving pieces: Straw hats, galvanized pails, and baskets.
Focal areas: Scarecrow, cornstalks, hay bales, refrigerator box outhouse.

Ship Ahoy Party

Outside: Row boat, cardboard pier with rope and life preservers.

Name Tags: Life preservers or sailboats.

Table coverings: Cover tables with blue cloths. For a "mast" attach a one-inch in diameter, three-foot long dowel rod to a two-by-four. Attach a white sheet "sail" to the mast. Place on table.

Centerpieces: Beach balls, sailor caps, life preservers, and seashells.

Focal areas: Wading pool with goldfish in water, float rafts, life preservers, beach balls, and plastic ducks. (Give the gold fish in a bowl to a preschool department.)

"I'm a Patriot" Party

Outside: Line a pathway with American flags or red, white and blue streamers attached to dowel rods.

Name Tags: U.S.A. map shapes or firecracker shapes with string "fuses" attached.

Walls, Ceilings, Doorways: Red, white, and blue helium-filled balloons. (Allow them to float to the ceiling.) Suspend garlands of gold and silver stars from doorways.

Table coverings: Fabric with stars-and-stripes motif.

Centerpieces: Make giant firecrackers by covering paper tubes with red construction paper; add white yarn for fuses. Cluster several "firecrackers" together.

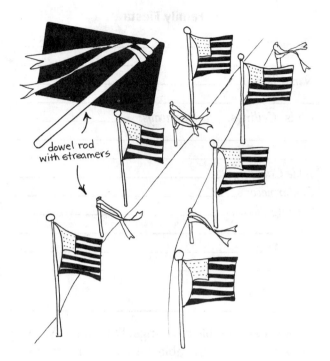

dowel rod with streamers

Table runners: Star garlands.

Serving pieces: Red plates, blue cups, white plastic utensils. Serve chips from "Uncle Sam" hats.

Back-to-School Party

Outside: Park a school bus outside with a banner saying, "A Good School Year or Bust."

Name Tags: Apple, book, or schoolhouse shapes.

Walls, Ceilings, Doorways: Display school pennants, chalkboards, and apple shapes, giant-size pencils, and tablets.

Centerpieces: Lunch boxes filled with apples, rulers, erasers, notebooks, crayons, and pencils.

Focal Areas: School desks, school supplies, pom poms, and school bell.

Around the World in Ninety Minutes

Outside: If possible, have children walk down a narrow hallway to the party room. Play sound effects from an airport. Give children "wings" and peanuts in individual packs as they enter.

Name Tags: airplane or suitcase shapes.

Walls, Ceilings, Doorways: World maps, travel posters of foreign cities, flags from around the world.

Table Coverings: paper maps (even maps of your city will give the effect needed).

Centerpieces: Souvenirs, globes surrounded by toy airplanes, canceled airline tickets.

Serving Pieces: Line small suitcases with plastic or foil and serve refreshments from them.

Spring Fling

Outside: Display large empty flower pots, potting plants, and a garden hose surrounded with a short picket fence.

Name Tags: Small plastic flower pots. Print names on the pots with permanent marker. Hang upside down around necks with thick yarn.

Table Coverings: Solid, bright colored cloths or flowered prints.

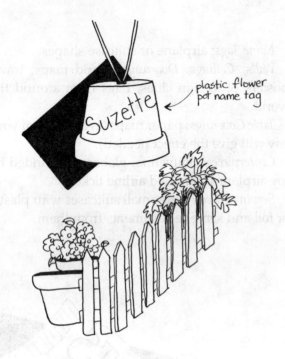
plastic flower pot name tag

Suzette

Family Fiesta

Outside: _____

_____

Name Tags: _____

Walls, Ceilings, and Doorways: _____

_____

Table Covering: _____
Centerpiece: _____
Serving pieces: _____

_____

Focal Area: _____

_____

Centerpieces: Potted plants, seed packets, small garden tools, watering cans.

Serving Pieces: Empty, clean flower pots.

Focal Areas: Wheelbarrows, flowerpots, seed packets, small potting plants, garden gloves, and small garden tools.

Do you have an idea of how to decorate to fit your party theme? Now, try your hand at planning decorations for a party. We'll give you a theme, and the rest is up to you!

Sources for table coverings: Do not use your family heirloom tablecloth at a children's party! Paper and plastic covering are available at many stores. Fabric remnants also make good, inexpensive tablecloths. In addition, consider using comic sections from the newspaper, or butcher paper to cover the tables. You may choose to use place mats made from large sheets of construction paper, pages from a wallpaper book, bandannas, or an opened pocket folder with napkin and utensils placed in pockets.

Hints for name tags: Name tags may be made in any shape from construction paper or other sturdy, colorful paper. Some objects lend themselves into being made into name tags. For instance: plastic lids, popsicle sticks, paper hats, small toys, large buttons, and puzzle pieces. Name tags may be hung around the neck, taped or safety pinned. Many commercially made name tags are available at party and card stores.

Where's a Good Place for a Fun Time?

Locations for children's parties and fellowships are all around. Consider a:
Fellowship hall
Classroom or department
Parking lot
Grassy area outside the church
Playground
Public park
Gymnasium
Local amusement park
Backyard
Church member's home
State park
Campground
Retreat center
Lake, beach, or river front
Church member's swimming pool
Pizza parlor or local restaurant
Neighboring church
Local school yard
Mall
Museum
Public or historical building

When taking children off the church premises, you will always need a permission slip. Extended activities (such as overnighters) call for a medical release form. Check your church policies and insurance stipulations regarding these forms. A lawyer could also provide your church with additional guidance regarding permission slips and medical forms.

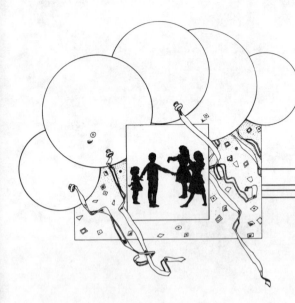

8
"What's There to Eat?"

Beyond Cookies and Punch

The child in all of us knows refreshments are the icing on the cake of a party! Who can resist cake and ice cream at a birthday party, cold watermelon after a summer picnic, or pink lemonade and cotton candy at the circus?

The sight and smell of food can call to memory fun times in our past. A fast-moving locomotive reminds us of a train cake an aunt made for us as children. And the smell of popcorn still brings to mind the happy movie nights for families presented in the fellowship hall. The refreshments we serve at parties may also help children have lasting memories.

Refreshments don't have to be expensive or fancy to appeal to children. Again, the rule is to be creative and fun. Even ordinary foods can become extraordinary when they complement the theme of a party.

Potato chips served in a glass punch bowl with Christmas lights sparkling beneath the bowl become "Salty Satellites" at an "Out-of-This-World" party. Peanut butter and strawberry jam sandwiches cut with a cookie cutter into heart shapes and served on paper doilies are "Heartbreakers" at a Valentine party.

When you have determined the theme, let your mind conjure up foods related to the theme or give names to the food chosen that will fit the theme. Think of inventive ways to present and serve refreshments.

As you determine a menu, remember:

• The time of the party. (Do you need to serve a full meal, breakfast, dessert, or a snack?)

• The time it will take to prepare the food, including shopping for the food.

• The children's likes and dislikes.

• The cleanup refreshments will make necessary.

• Your budget.

• Don't let refreshments conflict with a regularly scheduled meal!

When planning what refreshments to serve at a party, remember the age of the children. Meals are best served to older children. Snacks are appropriate for preschoolers and children alike.

Here are several never-fail, kid-pleasing foods to serve at your next party.

BOUNTIFUL BREAKFASTS

French toast	cinnamon sugar toast
A B C pancakes	doughnuts
individual boxes of cereal	

THE MAIN THING

hamburgers	hot dogs
corn dogs	pizza

sub sandwiches	sloppy joes
spaghetti	tacos

SENSATIONAL SNACKS

popcorn	nachos
Tater Tots	chips and dip
fruit and dip	vegetables and dip
watermelon	trail mix

DELIGHTFUL DESSERTS

cake	ice-cream cones
brownies	Popcicles
doughnut holes	popcorn balls
caramel apples	cotton candy
cookies	pudding

BETTER-THAN-AVERAGE BEVERAGES

fruit juices	ice water
chocolate milk	lemonade
fruit punch	soft drinks
hot chocolate	powdered drinks

Many refreshments are easy enough for children to prepare as a part of the party activities. Consider these:

Build a taco	No-bake cookies
Make S'Mores	Design a sundae
Squirt cheese on	Mix trail mix
celery and crackers	Decorate cookies
Create peanut butter	Rick Krispie treats
and jelly sandwiches	Roast marshmallows
Decorate cupcakes	Build banana splits

You may be looking for a different treat, a special something to serve at a party. If so, you'll enjoy these mouth-watering recipes. (Note: * indicates recipe could be prepared by children.)

Breakfast

Minimuffiins

1 package blueberry muffin mix
1½ cups powdered sugar
4 tablespoons orange juice

Prepare muffins according to directions on package. Bake in well-greased mini-muffin tins at 350°. Stir powdered sugar and orange juice to-gether to form a glaze. Dip warm muffins in the glaze before serving. (Makes 2 dozen.)

Wake-Up-Wrap-Ups*

½ pound mild sausage
1 can flaky biscuits

Preheat oven at 450° and lightly grease a cookie sheet.

Form balls of sausage about one inch in diameter. Cook in skillet until well-done. Drain on paper towels. Divide each biscuit in half. Wrap each cooked sausage in a patted-out half of biscuit dough. Bake for eight to ten minutes or until biscuit is golden brown. "Wake-Up-Wrap-Ups" may be frozen and reheated. (Makes 20)

Cinnamony Biscuits

1 can flaky biscuits
⅓ cup sugar
1½ teaspoons cinnamon
3 tablespoons melted oleo or butter

Heat oven to 425°. Separate biscuits and divide in halves. Mix sugar and cinammon in a small bowl. Dip each piece in melted butter and then roll in the sugar mixture. Place on lightly greased cookie sheet. Bake until golden brown.

Marvelous M & M Pancakes

2 cups pancake mix
1 cup milk
2 eggs
1 tablespoons oil
1 large package M & M's

Lightly grease and preheat an electric skillet. Combine first four ingredients, stirring until smooth. Spoon batter into hot skillet in small circles. When bubbles appear, sprinkle a few M & M's onto each pancake. Flip and cook a few more seconds. Serve immediately.

Orange Delight Toast

Small can of frozen orange juice

A buttered slice of bread for each person
Sugar to sprinkle on toast

Turn oven to broil. Butter bread slices and spread with one teaspoon frozen orange juice concentrate. Sprinkle with sugar. Broil until orange juice bubbles. Cool slightly before serving.

Batter-Up Sausage Balls

1 pound sausage
3 cups prepared dry biscuit mix
8 ounces shredded Cheddar cheese
3 tablespoons water

Preheat oven to 350°. Mix all ingredients together by hand. Form into one-inch balls. Bake for twelve minutes. Serve warm or at room temperature. (Note: "Batter-Up Sausage Balls" may be frozen and reheated for serving.) Makes a bunch!

Main Courses

High Seas Sandwiches*

3 medium-size cans of tuna
3/4 cup pickle relish
3/4 cup mayonnaise
12 hot dog buns

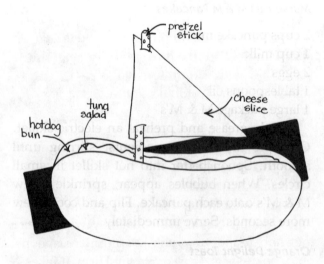

6 slices American cheese
Pretzel sticks

Mix together the first three ingredients. Spread the tuna mixture on the hog dog buns. Cut cheese diagonally, then fit each triangle of cheese on a pretzel stick to make a sail. Stick sails into tuna-filled bun boats. (Makes 12)

Petite Pizza Pleasers

1 pound mild ground sausage
1 pound processed cheese
2 loaves party rye bread
1 small can pizza sauce
1 bag shredded mozzarella cheese

Preheat oven to 375°. Brown sausage in skillet. Drain off grease. Combine processed cheese and browned sausage. When cheese is melted, add pizza sauce. Place rye bread slices on a cookie sheet. Spoon sausage mixture onto the bread and sprinkle with mozzarella cheese. Bake until mozzarella cheese is melted. Makes a bunch!

Oink-oink Corn Bread

1 8 1/2 ounce package corn bread mix
1 egg
1/3 cup milk
8 slices bacon

Preheat oven to 400°. Line the bottom of a nine-inch square pan with waxed paper and grease the pan and paper. Fry bacon until it is thoroughly cooked. Do not brown. Lay bacon on the waxed paper in the pan. Mix the first three ingredients and pour the batter over the bacon. Bake until golden brown. Remove from oven. Cool slightly before turning the corn bread out onto a serving plate. Remove the waxed paper. Cut into squares and serve warm. (Serves 8-10.)

Butterfly Sandwiches*

For each sandwich, cut a slice of bread in half diagonally. Spread one half with cream cheese and the other half with apple butter. Put the pieces together. Cut the sandwich again to form two small triangles. Arrange the triangles to resemble a butterfly. Place a carrot stick between the triangles to form the body of the butterfly.

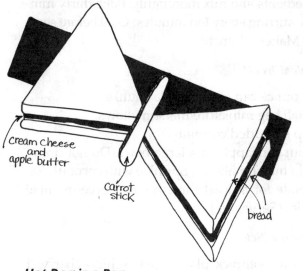

cream cheese and apple butter

carrot stick

bread

Hot-Dog-in-a-Bag

1 16-ounce loaf frozen bread dough, thawed
10 hot dogs
Mustard
Catsup

Preheat oven to 375° and lightly grease a cookie sheet.

Divide bread dough into ten equal parts.

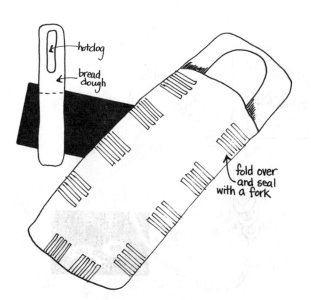

hotdog

bread dough

fold over and seal with a fork

Shape each dough piece into a rectangle about twice the size of a hot dog. Put a hot dog near one end of the dough. Fold the other end of the dough over three-fourths of the hot dog so it appears the hot dog is "resting" in a sleeping bag. Seal edges of the dough with a fork. Put each "Hot-Dog-in-a-Bag" on a cookie sheet and bake for fifteen minutes or until golden brown. Allow children to add mustard and catsup. (Makes 10.)

Hobo Stew

1 large can beef stew
1 can biscuits
1 cup shredded cheese

Preheat oven to 400°. Warm stew in a pan on the stove. Pour warmed stew in a baking dish. Place the biscuits around the edge of the dish and sprinkle with shredded cheese. Bake for ten minutes or until golden brown.

Snacks

Tooth Chippers

3 cups chocolate chips
2 cups miniature marshmallows
1 cup chopped walnuts

Melt chocolate chips in the top of a double boiler. Stir until smooth. Stir in marshmallows and walnuts. Pour the mixture into an eight-inch pan lined with aluminum foil. Let the candy stand until firm. Cut into squares.

Chompers

1/2 cup peanut butter
1 cup chocolate chips
1 cup salted peanuts

Heat peanut butter and chocolate chips in the top of double boiler. Stir constantly while melting. Add peanuts and stir. Drop from teaspoons onto cookie sheet. Refrigerate until firm. (Makes 2 dozen.)

Crunchies

2 6-ounce packages butterscotch chips
1 cup salted peanuts
2 cups chow mein noodles

Melt the butterscotch chips in the top of a double boiler. Stir in the peanuts and chow mein noodles. Drop mixture by teaspoons onto waxed paper. Chill until firm. (Makes 3 dozen.)

Sesame Snakes*

1 package refrigerator biscuits
3 tablespoons melted butter or oleo
3 tablespoons sesame seeds

Preheat oven to 400° and lightly grease cookie sheet. Cut biscuits in half. Roll dough into "snake" shapes. Place all "snakes" on a cookie sheet. Brush with melted butter and sprinkle with sesame seeds. Bake until lightly browned. (Makes 20.)

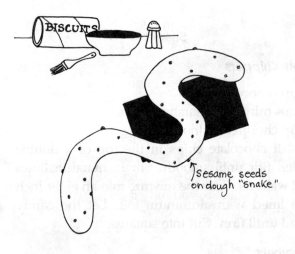

Sesame seeds on dough "snake"

Confetti

½ cup melted butter or oleo
1 envelope dry salad dressing mix
1 cup bite-sized shredded wheat
1 cup Cheerios
2 cups Rice Chex
2 cups salted peanuts
1 cup pretzel sticks

Preheat oven to 300°. Add dry salad dressing mix to the melted butter, mixing well. Combine all dry ingredients in a roasting pan or large baking dish. Pour the margarine mixture over the dry ingredients and mix thoroughly. Bake thirty minutes, stirring every ten minutes. Cool before serving. Makes a bunch!

Tropical Treat*

2 20-ounce can of pineapple chunks
1 small bag miniature marshmallows
1 cup shredded coconut

Pour pineapple in a large bowl. Do not drain. Stir in marshmallows. Sprinkle with coconut. Refrigerate for at least three hours. Serve in small bowls. (Serves 10.)

Fruit-on-a-Pick*

On a toothpick place 1 maraschino cherry, 1 pineapple chunk, and 1 miniature marshmallow. Eat!

Edible Jewelry*

2 cups Fruit Loops
⅔ cup round toasted oat cereal
4 rolls Lifesavers
8 pieces shoestring licorice

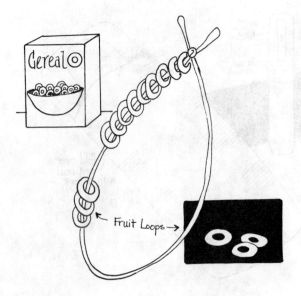

← Fruit Loops →

Tie a knot in the end of each piece of licorice. Open the rolls of Lifesavers and place the candy in a small bowl. Place each of the cereals in a separate bowl. Help the children string candy and cereal on the licorice to form an edible necklace. Tie the ends together so the necklace can be worn and eaten at the same time! (Makes 8.)

Chewy Snowballs

1½ ounces cream cheese at room temperature
1¼ cups sifted powdered sugar
Chopped nuts

Stir cream cheese with a wooden spoon. Gradually stir in powdered sugar. Form dough into balls and roll in chopped nuts. Refrigerate in a tightly covered container before serving.

Kaleidoscope Korn

10 cups popped popcorn
1 cup butter or margarine
¾ cup sugar
1 3-ounce package flavored gelatin
3 tablespoons water
1 tablespoon light corn syrup

Place popped corn in a large pan in a 250° oven to keep it warm. Butter bottom and sides of a large saucepan. Combine remaining ingredients and cook to hard ball candy stage (255°). The mixture *must* be stirred constantly. Pour mixture over popcorn and mix until all the popcorn is covered with the gelatin mixture. Bake in oven for five minutes. Remove from oven and stir. Bake another five minutes and then turn out on foil. Let cool. *Delicious!*

Pretzel Perfections

1 bag pretzels or pretzel sticks
1 cup raisins
2 cups round oat cereal
1 package of chocolate chips (Butterscotch chips or white chocolate may be substituted.)
1 cup pecans (optional)

Melt chocolate chips in the top of a double boiler. (Or melt chips in a large bowl in the microwave.) Add ingredients a few at a time to coat with chocolate and stir to cover with chocolate. Spread coated mix on a cookie sheet or foil to cool. Cool thoroughly and store in an air-tight container.

Desserts

Scripture Cake

1 cup Psalms 55:21
3 cups Jeremiah 6:20
6 Isaiah 10:14
3½ cups 1 Kings 4:22
1 teaspoon 1 Corinthians 5:6
½ teaspoon Leviticus 2:13
1 cup Genesis 24:17
1 teaspoon 1 Samuel 30:12
1 cup Numbers 17:8
1 teaspoon 1 Kings 10:10

Preheat oven to 325°. In a large bowl add one ingredient at a time following the instructions in Proverb 24's for making a good boy. Pour batter into a greased pan or into cupcake tins. Bake at 325° until a toothpick comes out clean. (It will take an hour or more for this large cake to bake.)

Note to adult leaders: Use a King James Version of the Bible. Look up each ingredient before the party to make sure you have it on hand.

Hole-in-One Sundae*

For each serving:
1 cake doughnut
1 scoop ice cream
Toppings: chocolate sauce, whipped cream, chopped nuts, and so on.

Place the doughnut in a bowl. Place a scoop of ice cream on the doughnut (making a hole-in-one!) Top as desired.

Ice-Cream Cone Cupcakes

Cake mix
24 flat-bottomed ice-cream cones
Canned frosting
Candy sprinkles

Preheat oven according to cake mix instructions. Stand cones on a cookie sheet. Mix cake according to instructions and fill each cone two-thirds full. Carefully place cookie sheet in the oven. Bake until inserted toothpick comes out clean. Cool completely before icing. Ice and top with candy sprinkles.

Everything's Coming Up Ice Cream!*

You will need one small clay or plastic flowerpot for each person. If flowerpots have holes in bottom, cover the inside of the pot with a piece of aluminum foil. Fill the flower pot with ice cream to within one-eighth of an inch of the top. Crush chocolate wafer cookies and sprinkle over the ice cream. (This becomes the "dirt.") Insert a clean, plastic flower into the ice cream. Freeze.

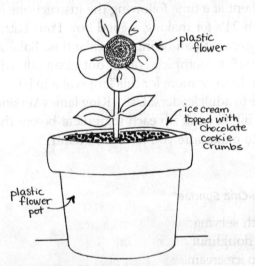

plastic flower

ice cream topped with Chocolate cookie Crumbs

plastic flower pot

Ice-Cream Cookiewiches*

Place a small dip of ice cream between two cookies to form a sandwich. Gently squish together. Store in the freezer. Set out a few minutes before serving to soften.

Hidden Treasure Cookies

Refrigerator cookie dough
1 bag miniature peanut butter cups

Preheat oven according to cookie instructions. Lightly oil miniature muffin pans. Roll teaspoons of cookie dough into balls. Place balls into muffin tin. Unwrap peanut butter cups and press one into each ball of cookie dough. Bake according to cookie package instructions. Cool thoroughly before removing from the pan.

Cherry Chart-Topping Tarts

3 8-ounce packages of cream cheese
1 cup sugar
4 beaten eggs
1 box vanilla wafers
Canned whipped cream topping
1 can cherry pie filling

Preheat oven to 350°. Line cupcake pans with aluminum cupcake liners. Mix together the first three ingredients. Place a vanilla wafer, flat side up, into each cupcake liner. Put a teaspoon of cherry pie filling on each wafer. Bake for twenty to twenty-five minutes. Remove from oven and cool for half an hour. Spread a teaspoon of cream cheese filling onto each tart. Add whipped cream topping before serving.

Mud Balls*

2 cups powdered sugar
1/2 cup cocoa
3/4 cup peanut butter
4 to 5 tablespoons water
1 1/2 tablespoons dry milk

Thoroughly mix all ingredients with your hands. Shape into small balls. Chill before serving.

Sombrero Sweets

1/4 cup butter
1/4 cup brown sugar

¼ cup sugar

½ teaspoon vanilla

½ teaspoon salt

1 egg

1 cup flour

½ cup quick-cooking oats

24 large marshmallows

Preheat oven to 375°. Lightly oil a cookie sheet. Beat butter until smooth. Add sugars. Stir in vanilla, salt, and egg. Add oats and flour. Drop cookies by teaspoon onto the cookie sheet. Flatten each cookie with the palm of your hand. Bake for eight minutes. Remove from oven and place a marshmallow in the center of each cookie. Bake for three minutes longer. (Makes 2 dozen.)

Zipper Bag Pudding*

1 package instant pudding mix

2 cups milk

1 large zipper bag

Place ingredients in the bag, sealing tightly. The children take turns squeezing the bag until the pudding is made. Spoon servings from the bag into ice-cream cones, cups, or bowls.

Bumpy Peanutty Treats*

1 cup creamy peanut butter

½ cup sweetened condensed milk

¼ cup powdered sugar

½ cup finely chopped salted peanuts

Blend peanut butter, condensed milk, and powdered sugar in a bowl. Mix with wooden spoon. Divide into one-inch balls. Roll balls in chopped peanuts. (Makes 2 dozen.)

Puddin'-on-a-Stick*

1 package instant pudding

2 cups milk

Wooden craft sticks

5 ounce paper cups

Combine pudding mix and milk. Stir until smooth. Pour into paper cups. Insert a stick into each cup of pudding. Place pudding cups in the freezer until frozen solid. Tear off the paper cup before eating.

wooden craft stick

5 oz. paper cup

Tasty Taffy

1⅓ cups sweetened condensed milk

½ cup molasses

⅛ teaspoon salt

Combine ingredients in heavy pan. Cook to the soft candy ball stage (255°). Remove from heat and pour into a buttered eight-inch square pan. Cool until candy can be handled. Show children how to pull the taffy between buttered fingers until candy is shiny and light-colored. Twist into a rope and cut into one inch strips.

Beverages

Chocolate Olé

8 cups milk

2 4-ounce milk chocolate bars

2 teaspoons cinnamon

2 teaspoons vanilla

Put milk and broken chocolate bars in a heavy pan. Cook over medium heat, stirring constantly until chocolate melts. Remove from heat and add remaining ingredients. Wouldn't this be great with "Sombrero Cookies?" (Serves 12.)

Summer Breeze Cooler*

Each child may make his own drink by placing two scoops of vanilla ice cream in a large paper cup. Pour two tablespoons of thawed orange juice concentrate over the ice cream. Fill the cup with lemon-lime carbonated beverage. Add a straw and drink up!

Icy Ideas

• Freeze a portion of your punch in ice cube trays so when they begin melting they do not dilute the punch.
• Put three Lifesavers in each ice cube section and fill with water. Float cubes in your party drink.
• Freeze food-colored water in a gelatin mold to make interesting shapes to float in punch. Dip the mold in warm water for a few seconds to help free the ice.
• Place fruit pieces (mandarin orange slices, canned pineapple chunks, cherries, and others) in ice cube trays or molds with water or juice and freeze.

Showers and Flowers Punch

1 quart of any flavor of sherbet
1 3-liter bottle lemon-lime soda
1 can whipped cream topping
Plastic flowers to garnish

Scoop sherbet into punch bowl and slowly add lemon-lime soda. Float plastic flowers in punch. As each glass is filled, add a cloud of whipped cream. (Serves 20.)

Raspberry Smoothie

2 10-ounce packages frozen red raspberries
1½ cups water
2 10-ounce bottles of lemon-lime carbonated beverage.

Partially thaw raspberries. Combine berries and water in a blender until smooth. Chill. Just before serving, add lemon-lime beverage. (Serves 12.)

Slushy Joy Juice

3 bananas, mashed
1 6-ounce can frozen orange juice concentrate
6 cups water
4 cups sugary flavor sherbet
46-ounces unsweetened pineapple juice
1 2-liter bottle lemon-lime carbonated beverage

Mix all ingredients except the lemon-lime beverage. Freeze in milk cartons until party time. Before serving, partially thaw the punch, and pour into serving bowl. Add lemon-lime beverage. Serves a bunch!

Heartwarmer Delight

6 cups apple juice
3 tablespoons red-hots
3 teaspoons lemon juice

Combine all ingredients in saucepan over low heat. Stir until red-hots are melted. Cool slightly before serving. (Serves 12.)

Dump Punch Ideas*

Some of the best party beverages happen without a recipe. Think of the flavors children like and then experiment! Try some of these ingredients in different combinations:

chocolate syrup	powdered drink mix
instant orange mix	flavorings and extracts
lemonade	carbonated drinks
fruit	instant cocoa
fruit juices	sherbet
honey	ice cream
milk	commercial fruit
vegetable juice	punches

Note: Remember to sip test as you mix!

Attention: Beware of food allergies! Outside your party room, list the foods and beverages you will be serving. Ask parents to notify you of any allergies their children have. Make appropriate substitutions for these special children.

Other Recipes to Try

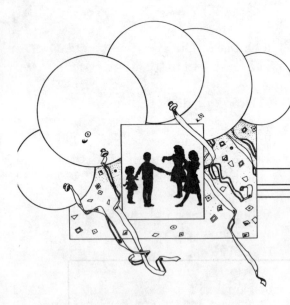

9
"How Was It?"

You Know You've Had a Good Time When . . .

How do you know when party goers have had a good time? You know they've had a good time when . . .

. . . boys and girls leave smiling.

. . . children do not want to leave.

. . . children immediately begin telling their parents about the party.

. . . sponsors say, "That was fun!" or "When do we do it again?"

. . . a parent calls and thanks you.

. . . you've had a good time yourself.

Often, but not always, you will experience these kinds of positive reactions to children's parties and fellowships. Actions and comments like these are good input for your evaluation.

But why should you evaluate your party? Evaluation helps you organize your thoughts about what was good, what worked well, what didn't work, and what you never want to do again at a party! In short, the evaluation process helps you plan better parties in the future.

Sources to Help with Evaluation

Ask yourself. Often we're our most critical evaluator. However, never lessen the importance of your own thoughts and feelings regarding any aspect of a party.

Ask the adult sponsors. Be sure to ask the other adults who assisted at the party to help evaluate. You may do this informally while cleaning up or over the phone. After an especially large party, you may wish to lead a debriefing session with adult leaders. Consider having them complete an evaluation form.

Ask the parents. Parents usually have a good idea of what was the best and the worst part of a party. These things become the topic of conversation while driving home in the car, eating supper, or preparing for bed. Ask: "What did Caleb like about the party?" "Was there anything Kelli didn't really enjoy at the party?" Accept the answers you receive and thank the parents.

Ask the children. Who better to ask than the children? Talk to them as they leave the party, call them on the phone, listen to their conversations. You will get much-needed, honest evaluation from boys and girls. When an annual party rolled around again, two children shared their favorite things that made the previous party "really neat!" Though it was long in coming, the evaluation was very useful.

Things to Evaluate

The theme. Was it appropriate and relevant? Did

the children relate to and enjoy the theme? Was it possible to make the various aspects of the party fit the theme?

The participants. Was the party well attended? Should others have been invited? Did the ages of the children affect the party? Did you have enough workers?

The schedule. Was it a good day for the party? Were there conflicts in scheduling? Was there enough time? Too much time? Was this party scheduled too close to the last party or fellowship?

The invitations and publicity. Was the publicity adequate? What else should have been done? Did the children receive the invitations in time to make plans to attend? Did the invitations tell the children (and parents) all they needed to know? Did they carry out the theme of the party?

The activities. Was there plenty to do? Were the children actively involved from the moment they arrived until they left? What was the most popular activity? What was least popular? Did the time seem to go by quickly, or did it "drag" in spots?

What learning took place? Did everyone participate? Did everyone feel a part of the group? Were they dangerous?

The decorations. How long did it take to set up? To clean up? Were the decorations interesting to the children? Was the expense reasonable? Did the decorations help to carry out the theme of the party? Did they add to the party atmosphere?

The refreshments. Were they good? Were they messy? Was the shopping and preparation time reasonable? How expensive were the refreshments? Did you calculate the amount needed accurately, or at least close? Would you serve them again? How much time did it take to clean up after refreshments? Did the children enjoy them? Did they ask for seconds? Did they go along with the theme of the fellowship?

Take the information you gather and file it. As a matter of fact, keep a file on every party you lead—start to finish. Files will help you when it is time to plan another fellowship.

Evaluate! You'll be glad you did!

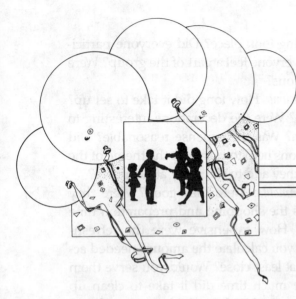

10
"Can You Give Me Some Ideas?"

4 Complete Fellowship Plans

Here are four of our favorite parties. You can use them exactly as written. Better yet, you can adapt them to meet the needs, interests, and likes of children in your church!

═══════════ ○ ═══════════

THEME: Noah's Ark Party

PURPOSE: To provide an alternative to Halloween for preschoolers, children, and their families. To discover prospects for our church. To have fun.

SCHEDULING: October 31, 5:30-9:00

PARTICIPANTS: Preschoolers through adults of our church, prospects, and our community.

INVITATIONS/PUBLICITY: Print large posters of Noah's Ark on heavy white paper. Include date, time, location, activities included in the fellowship, and the name of your church. Posters may be colored by children or adults or may be left white. Posters can be displayed throughout the church, in area stores, and in schools.

Reduce the poster to fit on a 4- by 6-inch card and mail to preschoolers and children in the church two weeks before the party. The cards may also be mailed in a bulk mailing to the community.

Place articles in the religion page of your local newspaper (usually there is no expense), and see if radio stations will make a free public service announcement about the party. (A month's notice is usually needed.)

Place articles in your church newsletter and reserve the front cover of the newsletter for party advertisement the two weeks prior to the Noah's Ark Party. Make handouts about the party to distribute to children after church-sponsored events. Use hallway bulletin boards for advertisement too. Teachers can make individual calls to children inviting them to the party. Encourage each child and his family to bring unchurched families to the party with them.

Special instructions to include in all publicity: "We're Boarding Noah's Ark! Come join us October 31 at 5:30 PM. Come dressed as a person, animal, or anything else on the ark!" (Children and adults have come to this party as the ark door, raindrops, a rainbow, a bale of hay, the world's largest white rabbit, and every kind of animal imaginable!)

DECORATIONS: Convert a gymnasium, parking lot, or fellowship hall into a carnival. Take your clues for booth decorations from the activities listed in this chapter. In addition to being decorated, each booth also needs a sign displaying its name.

• Make an "ark" out of three refrigerator boxes taped end-to-end. Cut an ark door and portholes. Paint the sides of the ark with brown tempera to resemble wood. Cut large animals from butcher paper, paint, and display near the ark.

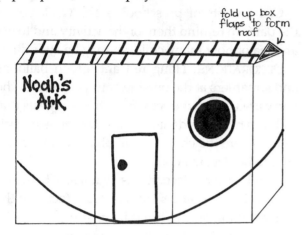

fold up box flaps to form roof

• Cover all tables with blue cloths to resemble water. Place plastic animals down the center of the tables.

• Create "Mr. Noah's Trick-or-Treat Hall" in one hallway of the church. Place bales of hay in the hall to form a maze to lead the children to four doors. Decorate the path from door-to-door by cutting animal footprints from brown adhesive-backed plastic and sticking the prints on the floor. (Don't forget to remove after the party!) Each door should be labeled with one of the following signs: Mr. and Mrs. Noah, Mr. and Mrs. Ham, Mr. and Mrs. Shem, Mr. and Mrs. Japeth.

Suspend raindrops cut from poster board and covered with aluminum foil outside the entrance to the hall. (Fishing line works well to hang the raindrops.) Plants, baskets, feed sacks, and other "ark items" can decorate the hallway also. Play a recording of animal sounds to set the mood.

Arrange for one adult in Bible costume to lead small groups of preschoolers and children through the hall periodically. The adult needs to give each child a small paper lunch sack for gathering treats. The children will knock on each door and be greeted by a couple in Bible costume. Each couple will greet the children and give them candy and a copy of a Bible verse.

REFRESHMENTS: Because of the hour of the party, many families will come without eating supper. Provide simple foods, such as hot dogs, nachos and cheese, corn dogs, frito pie, chili, cookies, soft drinks, apples, and hot chocolate. Make a banner above the food table that reads "Mrs. Noah's Kitchen." Over the drink table hang this sign: "Water Trough." You may wish to charge a small fee to help cover the expense of the food.

ACTIVITIES: Hang a banner at the entrance to the carnival games that reads "Noah's Arkcade." Have carnival prizes and candy to distribute. (One church collected candy from church members during the three weeks before the party and had so much given they were able to donate it to a local charity!) Here are some games and activities to use:

• Hand out helium-filled balloons
• Noah's track (tricycle race)
• Walk like the animals (sack races)
• Pony rides and petting zoo
• Ark ride (hayride)
• Duck pond (scoop a rubber duck from a wading pool and get a prize)
• Ark building (woodworking with scrap wood, hammers, nails, and glue)
• Feed the lion (bean bag toss into a "lion's" mouth)

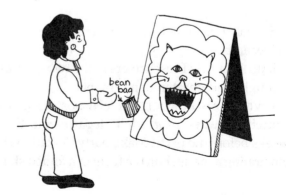

bean bag

- Shearing the sheep (removing shaving cream from inflated balloons with a plastic knife)
- Duck's delight (bobbing for apples)
- Survivors' swim (dunking booth)
- Gopher holes (miniature golf or croquet)
- Snap a memory (An instant photo booth set up in front of a rainbow. Charge seventy-five cents for each photo to cover the expense of the film.)
- Flood fishing (magnetic fishing for a prize)
- Three bear toss (wet sponges thrown at church staff members dressed as bears)
- Lightning throw (pitching cotton balls for distance)
- Patties-through-a-porthole (brown paper plates thrown through a target made from a tire hanging from a tree)
- Costume parade (use age-group categories and give prizes to everyone)
- Door prizes (Provide three to six nice door prizes—ranging from a children's puzzle to a Polaroid camera—and ask everyone who attends the party to register for a door prize. Have a drawing at the end of the party. Save all the entry cards and look through them for the names of unchurched preschoolers, children, and parents who might be prospects for your church!)

THEME: Jesus' Birthday Party

PURPOSE: To provide a learning and fellowship time. To allow parents a morning for Christmas shopping.

SCHEDULING THE EVENT: A Saturday morning in December.

PARTICIPANTS: Preschoolers in the two-year-old through kindergarten departments.

INVITATIONS/PUBLICITY: Place posters in the church hallways near adult departments three weeks before the party. Make party invitations by illustrating a manger on the front of a folded sheet of construction paper and putting party information inside the card. Place a few pieces of hay or straw inside the invitation before mailing. Mail invitations to children two weeks before the party.

Call parents of preschoolers the week before the party to remind them of the activity and to get an idea of how many children may be attending.

DECORATIONS: Hang red and green balloons and streamers at the outside entrance nearest the party area. Since the activity section suggests that children be divided into groups by their age, each room where the children will play, eat, and learn should be decorated also.

Avoid secular decorations (Santas, Christmas trees, reindeers, and so on.) Instead, focus on the true meaning of Christmas by displaying a nativity scene and pictures of the annunciation and birth of Jesus, the shepherds, and the Wise Men. Balloons and streamers can be used to carry through with the birthday theme in each room.

Prepare a room for the children to share their play. (See "Activities.") Place a manger filled with hay at the front of the room. Hide a doll nearby. Divide the rest of the floor space into four sections using masking tape. Label each section with one of the following words: *Stars, Angels, Sheep, Shepherd.* Ask two adults to dress as Mary and Joseph and ask another adult (perhaps the pastor) to serve as the play's narrator. Ask the adults to wait near the room until it is time for the play.

REFRESHMENTS: Serve birthday cake or cupcakes and fruit juice. You may wish to let preschoolers mix the cupcake batter as one of their activities. Place the cupcakes in a toaster oven to bake (make sure the toaster oven and its cord are out of the reach of children.) Allow the children to decorate the cupcakes before eating.

Another simple refreshment plan is to invite parents to bring a dozen cupcakes or cookies to share.

ACTIVITIES: Since the age and abilities of the

preschoolers will be different, divide them by age into four groups. Activities may include: making refreshments, making a Christmas ornament, hearing the Christmas story, singing Christmas songs, caroling in the hallways, making Christmas cards, moving to Christmas music.

Give each of the four groups one of the following assignments: stars, angels, sheep, shepherds. The preschoolers will play these parts in the play that follows. The children may make something to represent their part as one of the activities, for instance:

Stars—allow two-year-olds to cover precut cardboard stars with aluminum foil and carry them in the play. Practice saying, "Twinkle, twinkle, twinkle."

Angels—three-year-olds can make halos from gold or silver Christmas garland. Practice saying, "Jesus is born."

Sheep—make sheep ears from paper plates covered with cotton balls. The ears may be tied on the four-year-old children's heads with yarn. Practice saying, "Baa, baa, baa."

Shepherds—fives can make shepherd staffs from wrapping paper tubes. Practice saying, "Let's find Jesus."

Note: The play is not intended for performance before adults. Rather, it is a way for preschoolers to participate in, and learn about, the Christmas story.

Play: Jesus Is Born

(As children enter the room, direct each group, and their teachers, to sit in the area designated for them by the signs. Explain that as the story characters are introduced, each group will move and sit by the manger.)

Narrator: Long, long ago, Mary and Joseph went on a long trip to Bethlehem. Mary was going to have a baby.

Clippity-clop, clip-clop, clippity-clop, clip-clop went the donkey as Mary and Joseph traveled to Bethlehem.
(Mary and Joseph enter.)

Narrator: When Mary and Joseph got to Bethelehem, Mary was very tired. Joseph wanted to find a nice place for him and Mary to stay and rest. There was no place to stay. There was no room in the inn.

Joseph: "Mary, there is no place for us to stay. We will have to stay in the barn with the animals."

Mary: "The barn will be fine, Joseph. It will keep us warm. We can sleep on the hay."

Narrator: Donkeys and horses, cows and goats, sheep and ducks filled the barn. It was a dark, smelly place. But Mary and Joseph were glad they had found a place to stay. Soon it was night. Beautiful stars twinkled in the sky.
(Stars move to the manger saying, "Twinkle, twinkle, twinkle.")

Narrator: During the night, Baby Jesus was born. *(Mary gets the doll and holds it.)* Mary wrapped the baby in swaddling clothes and laid him in a manger. The manger, filled with hay, was Jesus' bed.

Outside Bethlehem, shepherds were taking care of their sheep in the fields. A bright light woke the sleeping shepherds. In the sky was an angel!

The angel said, "Don't be afraid, shepherds, I have good news for you. God's Son, Jesus, has been born in Bethlehem."

The shepherds were excited by the news. "Let's find Jesus," they said, and they ran to Bethlehem.

(Shepherds move saying, "Let's find Jesus," and the sheep move saying, "Baa, baa, baa.")

Narrator: The angels sang, "Glory to God in the highest. And on earth, peace, goodwill to all."

(Angels move, saying, "Jesus is born!")

Narrator: It was a special night when Jesus was born. The stars knew it. The sheep knew it. The shepherds knew it. And the angels knew it. I know it too. Don't you?

(Lead the preschoolers to sing "Away in a Manger." Narrator closes in prayer.)

THEME: B*A*S*I*C Training

PURPOSE: To help children learn some qualities of Christian heroes while having a fun time.

SCHEDULING THE EVENT: All day Saturday.

PARTICIPANTS: Fourth-sixth graders.

INVITATIONS/PUBLICITY: Use red ink to stamp the front of 9 by 12-inch manila envelopes "TOP SECRET." Place the following invitation inside the envelopes:

You are ordered to rendezvous with the fourth, fifth, and sixth grade soldiers on Saturday, May 5, at 0900 hours for B*A*S*I*C training. We'll see what it takes to be a REAL hero. Bring your gear: Bible, notebook, and pencil. Uniform for the day: fatigues, camouflage clothes, or blue jeans. These orders are TOP SECRET—only the Commander-and-Chief in your home may know!

Mail the invitations two to three weeks before the party.

Place posters made from drab green poster board and camouflage wrapping paper. Display the posters in the halls at church frequented by fourth, fifth, and sixth graders. You may wish to place B*A*S*I*C Training messages in the church newsletter. Start four to five weeks before the party by stating the name of the party and nothing else. In the weeks that follow, give more and more information until all the information is revealed two weeks before the party.

DECORATIONS: Cover tables with camouflage paper cloths (from a party or card store.) You will find napkins and cups to match. Instead of using paper plates, consider using foil pie pans to give a military "feeling." Serving dishes may be large metal pots, pans, and dippers.

Place a pup tent and military cot in one part of the party area. Other military items may also be displayed, such as parachutes, American flags, backpacks, helmets, canteens, and so on. (Note: Do *not* use guns or other toy weapons as part of the decorations, or in any other way during the party.)

Adult sponsors may wish to dress as sailors, marines, or soldiers. A green T-shirt worn with blue jeans would be effective too.

Make "dog tag" name tags by cutting tags from heavy gray paper. Punch a hole at the top of each tag and string silver nylon ribbon through it to form the "chain." Children may print their names on the dog tags with a permanent black felt-tip marking pen before hanging them around their necks. (They can also print their "number" on the tags by using their birth date: 4-17-1979.)

Use green paint on butcher paper to make a large sign for the refreshment area. The sign should read: MESS HALL. Make another sign in the same way for the games area, reading: USO SHOW. Make another section of the room into a study area. Make a third sign reading: MANEUVERS.

REFRESHMENTS: Have a "Make-Your-Own Hero Sandwich Line." Serve potato chips and call them "Medals of Honor." Serve limeade or lemonade with green food coloring added. The drink may be called "R and R Punch." For dessert, serve pudding in individual cans, calling them "Rations." Make signs for each of the foods you serve by printing on white construction paper with green felt-tip marking pen. Display the appropriate sign by each food item.

Display one sheet of poster board and a felt-tip marking pen for each team (see "Activities.") These sheets will serve as tally boards for each team's points accumulated during the study portion of the fellowship.

ACTIVITIES: As children arrive, help them make their dog tag nametags. Randomly divide the children into two to four groups (depending on the number of children present.) Give each team a military name such as: cadets, G.I.'s, recruits, troopers. Send the teams to the MANEUVERS area instructing them to stay together as a team.

Give each team member a copy of the "Name a Hero" worksheet and a pencil. The team members may use their Bibles. Assign at least one adult to each team. The adult cannot give answers, but can give the children hints about where to look in their Bibles for information. Give the children twenty minutes to complete the activity. Award two points to each team for correct answers.

The teams' next assignment is to define, as a group, the word *hero*. The team must then decide how to share their definition. They may sing it, cheer it, act it out, or share in any other way. Fifty points will be awarded to each team that shares a definition. Every team member must participate in the sharing if the team is to score any points, however.

Counselors will lead children to complete a Bible search and a "Hero Word Search." Bibles, pencils, and worksheets are needed. A team that looks up all the verses and finds all eighteen words in twenty minutes will score another fifty points (15-17 words scores 40, 10-14 scores 20, and 1-9 scores 10.) Allow the children to share the Bible verses and words before proceeding to the next activity.

Ask each counselor to take his or her group to a part of the room where they will be away from others. Each individual on a team may privately complete the sheet "Personal Inventory—Do I Know God?" with the counselor's guidance. A child may fold the sheet secretly and place it in his pocket or shoe so others will not see it. The counselor may close the group time with prayer, asking God to help everyone on the team become a Christian hero.

Tally up the points for each team. The team with the most points may get in the MESS HALL line first. After refreshments, lead the children to participate in the "USO Show" (which is all fun and games!).

Suggested games and activities:
• Capture the flag
• Use a parachute to foster teamwork. Children will stand around the parachute, holding the edges. Give instructions such as:
• Raise your arms.
• Lower the parachute to the ground without bending your knees.
• Crawl under the parachute without letting go with either hand.
• Set up an indoor or outdoor obstacle course.
• Use maps and/or a compass to help children get to another location or to find a hidden, coded message.
• Conclude by distributing medals for distinguished service to the children to reward them for "working to become Christian heroes." The medals may be made by gluing ribbon to a safety pin. Call each child by name and pin the medal to his outer clothing.

NAME A HERO

Work with your assigned group and counselor to see if you know which Bible character each statement below describes. You may use your Bible if you need to (and if you can get to it!) Each correct answer is worth two points.

HERO	ACTION
1. _____	This young woman was chosen to be the mother of Jesus.
2. _____	He was baptized in the Jordan River by John the Baptist.
3. _____	He escaped over a city wall in a basket.
4. _____	He wrote a letter to Timothy from prison.
5. _____	She traveled from Moab to Bethlehem with her mother-in-law.
6. _____	Her husband and two sons died in Moab.
7. _____	The grandfather of King David.
8. _____	He helped a poor widow when her son died.
9. _____	His three friends were thrown into a blazing furnace when they refused to worship an idol.
10. _____	He warned the people that their wickedness would lead to destruction.
11. _____	A tax-collector whose life took a turn for the better after Jesus ate with him.
12. _____	He took on the responsibility of marrying his fiancee even though she was pregnant (and the baby was not his!).
13. _____	He had a vision in the Temple, and he volunteered to serve the Lord.
14. _____	He was trained by Eli to do God's work.
15. _____	He took twelve stones and built and altar.
16. _____	He did not want to obey God at first. So he got on a ship and was later thrown overboard.

HERO	ACTION
17. _____	He was offered as a sacrifice by his father, but God spared him.
18. _____	He led the Israelites out of Egypt.
19. _____	He was ordained as a preacher in the church at Ephesus.
20. _____	He was a doctor, apostle, and author of two New Testament books.
21. _____	He was a shepherd, musician, and king.
22. _____	He became the first traveling missionary.
23. _____	He was a New Testament prophet who pointed the way to Jesus' coming (also Jesus' cousin).
24. _____	God promised He would begin a great nation through this man and that the whole world would be blessed because of the man.
25. _____	He was sold by his brothers.
26. _____ _____	Name two sets of brothers who were fishermen but gave up fishing to follow Jesus.
27. _____	He was somewhat impatient and always wanted to be first, but was trained by Jesus to do His work. (Known as the "rock.")
28. _____	God gave him a plan to defeat the Midianites with only 300 Israelite soldiers.
29. _____	His long hair gave him strength.
30. _____	He was wise and wealthy and built the Lord's Temple.
31. _____	He was a good king and led in the repair of the Temple.
32. _____	Abraham's wife, who gave birth to the beginning of a great nation.
33. _____	He got the birthright from his father through a trick.
34. _____	He led the people into the Promised Land.
35. _____	He prayed morning, noon, and at night. He also chose to eat good food.
36. _____	He was the king's cupbearer, and rebuilt the walls of Jerusalem.

37. _____ She was a strong woman who judged and encouraged her nation to do its best. The only woman prophet.

38. _____ She was a queen and risked her life to save her people.

39. _____ She was an active woman and helped Jesus feel comfortable in her home.

40. _____ Known as the "woman who sold purple," she was a leader in the early church.

41. _____ Jesus used her generous gift as an example to others of how to give.

42. _____ He brought the boy to Jesus who had a lunch that fed 5,000.

43. _____ He was leader of the church in Jerusalem and gave up his life rather than be unfaithful to Jesus.

44. _____ He was a tax-collector when he became a disciple of Jesus.

45. _____ He came to blind Saul at God's command, healed him, and helped him begin his ministry.

46. _____ He was a missionary, an assistant to Paul, and was known as an encourager.

47. _____ He wrote the second book in the New Testament.

48. _____ They were tentmakers and used their home to help Paul and other Christians.

49. _____ He died on the cross for us.

50. _____ He built an altar and prayed to God after the Flood.

PERSONAL INVENTORY
DO I KNOW GOD?

Often our actions will show whether we know God or not. Read the statements below. Check the answer for each statement that best describes you.

	Always	Sometimes	Never
I read my Bible daily.	____	____	____
I pray to God daily.	____	____	____
I go to church on Sunday.	____	____	____
I attend Sunday School.	____	____	____
I try to learn from my teachers, pastor, parents, and others.	____	____	____
I remember a time when I asked Jesus to be Lord and Savior of my life.	____	____	____
I let God help me make choices.	____	____	____
I share about God with others.	____	____	____
I want to know more about God.	____	____	____

Assignment: Circle three of the above statements you are going to work to improve, *beginning* this week. Share what you are going to work on with others in your group.

Pray: Right now stop and pray for one another. Each of you may choose one person in your group to pray for. Ask God to help that person make the changes or improvements they mentioned. Remember: Prayer requests are special things that friends do *not* share with others.

Next: When your group is finished, sit and talk quietly while the other groups finish.

HERO WORD SEARCH
Find 18 words!

```
A C C P E N S O N I C F Y N T
Z B H D G I H J E V E I L E B
L N O A R Q F T W A U K P M S
B E D F N H I O K M C J G L A
T N R V P G Q H L Y O X S U W
C K M Z A I E G N L O E J B L
T V P U L S F D O T O W Q D R
W N C A O Z Y E G H X W F B D
J Q E P V S I Y N L R T K M O
W Y V I E U L E A R N X A Z T
K C S F T I B X M V A Q D O T
W U G N T A J E Z R L H A P E
O B E Y B F P D G I H E S N V
U P A R O C Q T E L K M E T I
D U S E E Y J A U Y O E R W G
I A E R C N D F G V O F V K R
S Q U M B T E E H U I J E L O
C P O P R C S Y X G A W I Z F
I A O E A J C D Q F A H L N K
P Q S E B O T P Y A E U M B W
L C P S E L F - C O N T R O L
I E R F D H K M Z L V G X J I
N P O S R N W I T N E S S E S
E K Q U T A E C F A B D H G I
D I S T J R M C C A L L E D R
W N V E K Z O D N E O O P Q I
X D F H L Y A N B E O G U T J
A K N L M Q E R G P P B Z V X
O C H R I S T I A N S W A Y C
```

Hint: The words may be written vertically, horizontally, diagonally, *and* backward!

Look at the verses below. Find a key word in the verse that is a characteristic a Christian hero should possess. Write the word in the blank by the verse reference on this sheet. Find the word in the Word Search and circle it.

Word Search Verses

Mark 12:31 _____
Genesis 25:27 _____
Acts 1:8 _____
John 8:12 _____
Colossians 3:22 _____
John 6:36 _____
Ephesians 4:32 _____
Psalm 100:2 _____
James 5:8 _____
2 Peter 1:6 _____ - _____
1 Corinthians 11:32 _____
Ephesians 5:10 _____
Matthew 5:8 _____
Psalm 27:14 _____
Acts 26:28 _____
1 Samuel 3:5 _____
1 Corinthians 15:51 _____
Matthew 6:14 _____

What heroic Christian characteristics do you have? List three below:
_____
_____

What three heroic characteristics do you need to develop? List them:
_____
_____

PRAY: Thank God for your good heroic characteristics. Ask God to help you develop the characteristics you listed.

THEME: Family Fiesta

PURPOSE: To provide a fellowship as part of Vacation Bible School family night. To meet and greet prospects.

SCHEDULING THE EVENT: If you have Vacation Bible School during the day, schedule this event one night during the Vacation Bible School; if you are having a night Vacation Bible School, consider having the event on the Saturday following the school, 6:00 to 8:00 PM.

PARTICIPANTS: All preschooler and children who have attended Vacation Bible School and their families, VBS teachers, and the church as a whole.

INVITATIONS/PUBLICITY: Advertise the Family Fiesta to your church simultaneously with Vacation Bible School. Make a different handout to send home with children each day of Vacation Bible School preceding the Family Fiesta. The invitations should be printed on bright paper (organge, fuchsia, or fluorescent yellow, for instance.)

Place a small drawing of a pinata, sombrero, or other Mexican object on the invitation before printing. You may even find self-adhesive stickers to enhance the invitations. The day of the party, send each child home with an invitation sealed in an envelope. (Before sealing the envelope, place a teaspoon of colorful confetti inside!)

DECORATIONS: Plan to use a large room or gymnasium. Let your imagination go wild as you begin to decorate!

You may hang multicolored streamers throughout the room (bright colors are better than pastels). Fold-out, tissue paper starbursts are also good additions. Have pinatas (available from party, gift, or import stores) throughout the room. Gather sombreros, ponchos, and other Mexican items from church members. Display them throughout the room.

confetti

Cover each serving table with a bright fabric cloth of a different color. Make an arrangement of terra cotta clay pots to hold serving utensils. The terra cotta flowerpot trays make good serving dishes. Place a miniature cactus on each table. Spread handfuls of confetti down the center of each table.

Encourage children, teachers, and parents to dress in Mexican costumes, madras plaids, peasant blouses and full skirts, or other bright clothes.

REFRESHMENTS: One church found an authentic Mexican bakery nearby and ordered various Mexican desserts to serve with fried ice cream and soft drinks. You might want to have the ingredients for party goers to build tacos or burritos. A potluck Mexican dinner would be a good way to get everyone involved and keep the expenses down.

ACTIVITIES: Invite a Mexican cultural preservation group, a Spanish band, or guitarist to entertain. You could play recorded music. Allow ample time for mixing and mingling. Since prospects will be present, you will want church members to have an opportunity to introduce themselves and to visit. Make sure you plan a time for the breaking of pinatas. You need an open space, a blindfold, a stick or plastic baseball bat, children, and pinatas filled with candy and small prizes.

Ask your pastor to lead a brief worship devotional in the church sanctuary. Ask families to sit together during the service.

Conclude activities with an open house in each of the Vacation Bible School departments. Teachers, children, and parents will want to visit and see what the children have learned and done.

11
"More Ideas?"

100 More Party Ideas

(Page numbers for the titles in bold are given in the index.)

THEME: ABC, 1-2-3
SCHEDULING: Just prior to new school year
PARTICIPANTS: New kindergarteners
INVITATIONS: Deliver M & M's with invitations.
DECORATIONS: Decorate tables with ABC blocks. Fill open lunch boxes with "school things," large beginners' pencils, erasers, rolled drawing paper, and so forth.
REFRESHMENTS: **Marvelous M & M Pancakes** and milk
ACTIVITIES: **The Great Alphabet Adventure.** Give each team an adult helper.

THEME: Adopt-a-Grandparent Valentine Party
SCHEDULING: February 14
PARTICIPANTS: Senior adults and fourth through sixth-graders
INVITATIONS: Heart-shaped cards
DECORATIONS: Red, white, and pink streamers on red and white tablecloths Lots of red paper hearts cut from construction paper
REFRESHMENTS: **"Heartbreaker" sandwiches, Heartwarmer Delight**
ACTIVITIES: Go to a nursing home and host the Valentine party. Make Valentines before going to the nursing home.

THEME: Apple Bash
SCHEDULING: Any summer or fall day
PARTICIPANTS: Grades one through three
INVITATIONS: Big red apple shape
DECORATIONS: Red, yellow, and green apples, green and white streamers.
REFRESHMENTS: Peanut butter with apple jelly, chilled apple juice.
ACTIVITIES: Apple relay, longest apple peeling (players will use a butter knife to peel apples.)

THEME: April Showers Bring May Flowers Party
SCHEDULING: Last Saturday in April
PARTICIPANTS: Fourth to sixth graders
INVITATIONS: Umbrella shaped
DECORATIONS: Umbrellas hung upside down and filled with big tissue paper flowers
REFRESHMENTS: **Everything's Coming Up Ice Cream, Showers and Flowers Punch**
ACTIVITIES: **Musical Breeze Chimes,** pot flowers and take to senior adults.

THEME: Around the World in Ninety Minutes
SCHEDULING: During special missions emphasis

PARTICIPANTS: Grades one through six
INVITATIONS: Globe shape
DECORATIONS: Pictures of different nationalities, curios from other countries
REFRESHMENTS: **Petite Pizza Pleasers**
ACTIVITIES: Read books about missionaries; have a missionary speak. Have a person from another country speak to the group about how his country is different from ours.

THEME: Bibles, Beach Balls, and Butterflies
SCHEDULE: Summer
PARTICIPANTS: Grades four to six
INVITATIONS: Bibles, beach balls, or butterflies—or all three
DECORATIONS: Hang beach balls with string from the ceiling. Make Bibles and butterflies from boxes and hang them also.
REFRESHMENTS: Butterfly Sandwiches (p. 00) lemonade
ACTIVITIES: **"Wet Tug-of-War,"** play "Keep Away" with a beach ball.

THEME: Bible Families Fellowship
SCHEDULE: A summer Sunday evening after church
PARTICIPANTS: The whole family
INVITATIONS: Open Bible
DECORATIONS: Pictures of Bible families
REFRESHMENTS: **Ice cream Cookiewiches, Dump Punch**
ACTIVITIES: **Creative Crayon Family Crest,** Make Bible family trees.

THEME: Bible Olympics
SCHEDULE: Saturday morning
PARTICIPANTS: Kindergarten—sixth graders
INVITATIONS: Torch shape
DECORATIONS: Hula hoops to represent Olympic rings, sports equipment, red, white, blue streamers

REFRESHMENTS: **Fruit-on-a-Pick,** Summer Breeze Cooler
ACTIVITIES: **Shape-Up,** relays, and obstacle courses

THEME: Bike Rodeo
SCHEDULING: Summer morning or Saturday
PARTICIPANTS: Bike riders
INVITATIONS: Picture of bicycle on front
DECORATIONS: Since this will be outside, decorations as such are not necessary. It would be good to use yellow or orange cones to mark off the area.
REFRESHMENTS: Sack lunches with trade-offs. (Allow 2 minutes for participants to "swap" items out of their lunches!)
ACTIVITIES: Bicycle safety, relays, obstacle course, decorate bikes

THEME: Boys' Cookie Bake-Off
SCHEDULE: Sunday night after church
PARTICIPANTS: First- through sixth-grade boys
INVITATIONS: Cookie shaped
DECORATIONS: Cover tables with blue cloths
REFRESHMENTS: Boys bake cookies at home and bring to share. **Dump Punch**
ACTIVITIES: Panel of judges will award ribbons of some kind to every cookie baker!

THEME: Bright Idea Bash
SCHEDULE: While adults are in a special study
PARTICIPANTS: First through sixth grades
INVITATIONS: Light bulb shape
DECORATIONS: String twinkle lights outside and on the party room ceiling.
REFRESHMENTS: Fix-your-own banana split
ACTIVITIES: **Do You Buy That?** Give each team a pile of supplies and let them "invent" something.

THEME: Cartoon Caper
SCHEDULING: Saturday morning

PARTICIPANTS: Preschoolers/children (choose an age group and plan accordingly).
INVITATIONS: Put an index card inside comic strip and print invitation on card
DECORATIONS: Cover table with comic section of newspaper
REFRESHMENTS: **Orange Delight Toast,** cold milk, or juices
ACTIVITIES: Watch a Disney movie especially chosen by teachers.

THEME: Catch a Wave Party
SCHEDULE: Summer
PARTICIPANTS: Fourth through sixth grades
INVITATIONS: Draw waves on outside of folded invitation with blue felt-tip pen.
DECORATIONS: Beach towels, beach umbrellas, lawn chairs
REFRESHMENTS: Soft drinks, chips, and dips
ACTIVITIES: **Water Balloon Fights,** go to a church member's swimming pool.

THEME: Cereal Serial—Bring a Friend for Breakfast and Movies
SCHEDULE: Saturday morning
PARTICIPANTS: Elementary children
INVITATIONS: Write a message with some of the words written with alphabet cereal or noodles.
DECORATIONS: Advertisements of cereal, empty cereal boxes, empty milk cartons
REFRESHMENTS: Individual boxes of cereal, milk, fruit.
ACTIVITIES: Watch nonviolent cartoons. Discuss cartoons after seeing them.

THEME: Christmas-Around-the-World Holiday Hunt
SCHEDULE: Saturday in December
PARTICIPANTS: Younger children
INVITATIONS: Globe-shaped ornament
DECORATIONS: Gloves, maps, wrapped packages, pictures of Christmas celebrations in other countries, lots of streamers!
REFRESHMENTS: Goodies from around the world
ACTIVITIES: Study Christmas traditions of other countries. Play games played by children in other countries.

THEME: Collections, Cookies, and Crazy Times
SCHEDULE: April Fool's Day
PARTICIPANTS: Grades one through six
INVITATIONS: Deliver invitations with a cookie.
DECORATIONS: Tables to display "collections."
REFRESHMENTS: **Ice Cream Cookiewiches**
ACTIVITIES: Show off collections, tell jokes, and make Cookiewiches.

THEME: Color-Me-Happy Party
SCHEDULE: Some "Ho-Hum" day
PARTICIPANTS: Grades one through six
INVITATIONS: Happy face with a crayon enclosed, with information on one side about the party and instructions to make a happy face on the other.
DECORATIONS: Cardboard crayons, multi-colored tablecloths, happy faces
REFRESHMENTS: **Kaleidoscope Korn**

THEME: Community Helper Holiday
SCHEDULE: Saturday morning
PARTICIPANTS: Preschoolers
INVITATIONS: Fire truck
DECORATIONS: Hats or paper dolls of community helpers
REFRESHMENTS: Apple slices, banana chunks, bread and jelly sandwiches
ACTIVITIES: **Human Ticktacktoe.** Visit a fire station, write thank-you notes to community helpers. Have a community helper speak to the group on how they can help.

THEME: Corn Dog Catastrophe
SCHEDULE: Hot summer day
PARTICIPANTS: Preschoolers

INVITATIONS: On a corn dog shape
DECORATIONS: None needed
REFRESHMENTS: Corn dogs, cold milk
ACTIVITIES: Sprinkler fun

THEME: Country Doin's Shindig
SCHEDULE: Summer
PARTICIPANTS: Families
INVITATIONS: Make an invitation cover from gingham fabric
DECORATIONS: Bandanas, straw hats, bales of hay, buckets, baskets, and so on
REFRESHMENTS: Fried chicken legs, corn-on-the-cob, iced drinks
ACTIVITIES: Three-legged race, wheelbarrow race, sing-along with a guitarist

THEME: Cupcake Caper
SCHEDULE: Summer weekday.
PARTICIPANTS: Preschoolers
INVITATIONS: Printed on a cupcake liner
DECORATIONS: None necessary
REFRESHMENTS: **Ice-Cream Cone Cupcakes**
ACTIVITIES: Do what I do, listen to a story

THEME: Everybody's Birthday Bazaar
SCHEDULE: Everyone with a birthday in a three-month period
PARTICIPANTS: Children, grades one through six
INVITATIONS: Enclose a small birthday candle
DECORATIONS: Paper tablecloths, hats, balloons, streamers
REFRESHMENTS: Cake!
ACTIVITIES: **Silent Birthday Hunt**

THEME: Everybody Have a Ball
SCHEDULE: Friday Night
PARTICIPANTS: Family
INVITATIONS: Baseball shape
DECORATIONS: Not needed
REFRESHMENTS: **Batter-up Sausage Balls**
ACTIVITIES: Attend or play a ball game.

THEME: Excavation Extravaganza
SCHEDULE: Saturday morning
PARTICIPANTS: Preschoolers
INVITATIONS: Treasure chest
DECORATIONS: Shovels, sand in a child's wading pool with treasure to dig
REFRESHMENTS: **Hidden Treasure Cookies**
ACTIVITIES: **Refreshment Treasure Hunt**

THEME: Family Circus Under the Big Top
SCHEDULE: Saturday
PARTICIPANTS: Families
INVITATIONS: Circus tent shape
DECORATIONS: Use a big tent or three smaller ones; one for refreshments, one for games, one for devotions
REFRESHMENTS: **Confetti,** cotton candy
ACTIVITIES: Elephant walk, any games or activities with a "circus" theme

THEME: Family Fiesta
SCHEDULE: Vacation Bible School Family Night
PARTICIPANTS: Families
INVITATIONS: Sombrero shape
DECORATIONS: Pinatas, sombreros, serape, clay pots
REFRESHMENTS: **Sombrero Sweets**
ACTIVITIES: Pinata break, go to open house in VBS rooms

THEME: Far-Out, Far-East Party
SCHEDULE: Breezy summer evening
PARTICIPANTS: Children, grades one through six
INVITATIONS: Deliver invitations in Chinese carry-out containers.
DECORATIONS: Paper lanterns, goldfish in bowls
REFRESHMENTS: Fortune cookies, Chinese foods to sample
ACTIVITIES: Chinese tag

THEME: Father/Daughter Night
SCHEDULE: Weeknight

PARTICIPANTS: Fathers/daughters (or other special man)
INVITATIONS: Flower corsage
DECORATIONS: Tables for four with flowers and pretty cloths, pastel streamers
REFRESHMENTS: **Raspberry Smoothie**
ACTIVITIES: Games where father and daughter can be partners

THEME: Father-and-Son Hike
SCHEDULE: All day Saturday
PARTICIPANTS: Fathers and sons (or other special man)
INVITATIONS: Hiking boot shape
DECORATIONS: None needed
REFRESHMENTS: Hot dogs, chips, cold drinks
ACTIVITIES: Hiking fun and talk, pick up litter

THEME: Festival of Booths
SCHEDULE: Summer morning
PARTICIPANTS: Preschool through second grade
INVITATIONS: Palm branches for a border
DECORATIONS: Bamboo, greenery, rugs and mats to sit on
REFRESHMENTS: Different kinds of fruit and raw vegetables
ACTIVITIES: Sing-along and storytelling

THEME: Follow the Clues: Find the Fun
SCHEDULE: Any time
PARTICIPANTS: Grades four through six
INVITATIONS: Map or footprints
DECORATIONS: Mail several "clues" about the fellowship
REFRESHMENTS: Keep it a secret!
ACTIVITIES: **Puzzle Partners**

THEME: Free-at-Last Blast
SCHEDULE: Saturday after the last day of school
PARTICIPANTS: All schoolchildren
INVITATIONS: Bird cage with door open and "Free at Last" printed on cage

DECORATIONS: Outside—none needed
REFRESHMENTS: hamburgers, chips, baked beans
ACTIVITIES: **Yes! The Glob**

THEME: Friendship Prescriptions
SCHEDULE: Saturday afternoon
PARTICIPANTS: Grades three through six
INVITATIONS: Handout at Sunday School with invitation rolled and placed in clean prescription bottle.
DECORATIONS: None needed
REFRESHMENTS: Plan to stop at a fast-food place for a treat.
ACTIVITIES: Take children to visit new members and prospects.

THEME: Game Shows and Good Times
SCHEDULE: Summer evening.
PARTICIPANTS: Grades one through six and parents
INVITATIONS: Gameboard shape
DECORATIONS: Lots of small tables and floor space for game playing.
REFRESHMENTS: Trail mix, **Crunchies, Confetti, Dump Punch**
ACTIVITIES: Several kinds of game-show games and board games

THEME: Girls Growing Gracefully Night
SCHEDULE: Sleep-over night when girls are out of school
PARTICIPANTS: Sixth grade girls
INVITATIONS: Silhouette of a young lady
DECORATIONS: Pink tablecloths, use hand mirrors, tape measures, pink nail polish, pink carnations in vases.
REFRESHMENTS: Lots of goodies. **Minimuffins**
ACTIVITIES: **Creative Crayon Placemats.** Have a qualified person show and tell the girls about personal hygiene and how to use makeup, watch posture, and so forth.

THEME: Go-Fly-a-Kite Fellowship
SCHEDULE: Windy day in April
PARTICIPANTS: Grades one through six
INVITATIONS: Kites with information on tail-pieces
DECORATIONS: Not needed.
REFRESHMENTS: Popcicles
ACTIVITIES: Make and fly kites. Make and **blow bubbles**

THEME: Good News Party
SCHEDULE: Saturday afternoon
PARTICIPANTS: Grades five and six
INVITATIONS: Written on newspaper
DECORATIONS: Construction paper signs with "Good news" posted all over the room!
REFRESHMENTS: Watermelon
ACTIVITIES: **Sidewalk chalk activities.** Lead a praise time, write cards to absentees, shut-ins, call a new member.

THEME: Good Ol' Days Party
SCHEDULE: Fall evening.
PARTICIPANTS: Grades three through six and parents
INVITATIONS: Wagon, buggy, or Model-T
DECORATIONS: Ol' time anything!
REFRESHMENTS: **Puddin'-on-a-Stick,** or home-made ice cream and cake.
ACTIVITIES: **Rubbed Memories** or any games your mama and daddy played—hopscotch, jump rope, marbles

THEME: Goofy Olympics
SCHEDULE: Any time!
PARTICIPANTS: Children and families.
INVITATIONS: Made from letters cut from a newspaper.
DECORATIONS: T-shirts, old tennis shoes, and so forth
REFRESHMENTS: **Petite Pizza Pleasers**

ACTIVITIES: Silly games or any game that you can change a little to make it "goofy!"

THEME: Greatest Pet Show on Earth
SCHEDULE: Summer, fall, or spring Saturday
PARTICIPANTS: Children and pets
INVITATIONS: Dog house, dog bone, or bird cage
DECORATIONS: None needed, but have area roped off for pet showing and for judges.
REFRESHMENTS: **Sesame Snakes**
ACTIVITIES: Show off pets in different categories and abilities. Give every participant a ribbon.

THEME: Hats! Hats! Hats!
SCHEDULE: Any time.
PARTICIPANTS: Preschool through second grade
INVITATIONS: Hats! Enclose pattern to make a hat.
DECORATIONS: Hats!
REFRESHMENTS: Serve fruit and peanut butter and crackers from plastic hats.
ACTIVITIES: Read the book, *Hats for Sale*. Have a hat parade, make hats.

THEME: Hawaiian Luau
SCHEDULE: Dead of winter
PARTICIPANTS: Grades three and four and families
INVITATIONS: Plastic lei with invitation attached
DECORATIONS: Hawaiian, of course!
REFRESHMENTS: **Tropical Treat**
ACTIVITIES: Table games, but play them on the floor

THEME: Hobbies and Hamburgers
SCHEDULE: A summer evening
PARTICIPANTS: Fourth through sixth graders
INVITATIONS: Send a packet of catsup with the invitation.
DECORATIONS: Picnic tables on a shady lawn
REFRESHMENTS: Hamburger cookout, home-made ice cream

ACTIVITIES: Everyone brings their favorite hobby to share.

THEME: Hobo Barbeque
SCHEDULE: Friday night
PARTICIPANTS: Families
INVITATIONS: Make a miniature hobo bundle with invitation enclosed
DECORATIONS: Anything hobo—fake campfire, bundles on sticks, tin cans
REFRESHMENTS: **Hobo Stew**
ACTIVITIES: A campfire sing-along

THEME: "I Can't Bear It" Fellowship
SCHEDULE: Morning
PARTICIPANTS: Preschoolers
INVITATIONS: Teddy bears
DECORATIONS: Bears! Bears! Bears!
REFRESHMENTS: Peanut butter and honey sandwiches
ACTIVITIES: **Strung-Out Scavenger Hunt**

THEME: "I Wanna Be" Party
SCHEDULE: Saturday or summer morning
PARTICIPANTS: Preschool through second grade
INVITATIONS: Send an assignment with the invitation that says: Complete this sentence: When I grow up I want to be _____ (Parent will need to write for preschoolers)
DECORATIONS: Hats, or objects easily identified with occupations
REFRESHMENTS: Fruit and vegetable snacks
ACTIVITIES: **My Secret Self,** share information on assignments.

THEME: "I'm a Patriot" Party
SCHEDULE: President's Day or Fourth of July
PARTICIPANTS: Grades one through six
INVITATIONS: Enclose a small flag
DECORATIONS: Flags, red, white, and blue bunting, gold star garlands
REFRESHMENTS: **Cherry Chart-Topping Tarts**
ACTIVITIES: A parade with flags and rhythm instruments

THEME: Intercontinental Contests
SCHEDULE: Evening
PARTICIPANTS: Children, grades one through six
INVITATIONS: On globe shape with map in background and invitation printed over it
DECORATIONS: Flags, maps, travel posters
REFRESHMENTS: Any "other continent" food
ACTIVITIES: **The Great Trade Off,** games children from other continents play.

THEME: It's-Under-Wraps Christmas Party
SCHEDULE: Three weeks before Christmas
PARTICIPANTS: Four-year-olds through sixth grade
INVITATIONS: Wrap invitations in wrapping paper
DECORATIONS: Not needed.
REFRESHMENTS: Bake cookies from frozen dough and decorate with premade frosting.
ACTIVITIES: Make family Christmas gifts, **Original Wrap-ups**

THEME: Jelly Bean Jamboree
SCHEDULE: Winter
PARTICIPANTS: First and second grades
INVITATIONS: Wrap a few jelly beans in plastic wrap and mail with invitation
DECORATIONS: Jelly-bean colored balloons
REFRESHMENTS: Jelly-bean decorated cupcakes, ice cream
ACTIVITIES: Jelly bean relay (carry on spoon); guess the number of jelly beans in a jar

THEME: Jesus' Birthday Party
SCHEDULE: Saturday morning near Christmas
PARTICIPANTS: Two-year-olds through sixth grade
INVITATIONS: Lamb, cake, or star
DECORATIONS: Balloons, hats, streamers
REFRESHMENTS: Cake, ice cream
ACTIVITES: **Fun with Dough;** read Luke 2, act out the Christmas story

THEME: Jogging Jubilee
SCHEDULE: Saturday, 8:00 AM
PARTICIPANTS: Grades one through six, parents
INVITATIONS: Tennis shoes
DECORATIONS: Not needed
REFRESHMENTS: Make your own sandwich, fruit
ACTIVITIES: Mark off a jogging route.

THEME: Jungle Party
SCHEDULING: Any time
PARTICIPANTS: Preschool through second grade
INVITATIONS: Lion shape
DECORATIONS: All kinds of stuffed "jungle animals"
REFRESHMENTS: **Tropical Treat,** bananas dipped in chocolate and frozen
ACTIVITIES: Upset the jungle basket—using jungle animal names, elephant walk

THEME: Let's Go Zooing
SCHEDULE: All day
PARTICIPANTS: Preschoolers, children, and adult sponsors
INVITATIONS: Animal shapes
DECORATIONS: None needed
REFRESHMENTS: Sack lunch to eat in park, lemonade
ACTIVITIES: **Two-by-Two,** visit a zoo

THEME: Lunar Launch
SCHEDULE: Friday night
PARTICIPANTS: Children, grades three through six
INVITATIONS: Stars
DECORATIONS: String twinkle lights outside and on the party room ceiling
REFRESHMENTS: Fill cones with ice cream and turn upside down to form "rockets."
ACTIVITIES: **Moonlight Volleyball**

THEME: Mirror Reflections
SCHEDULE: Late morning
PARTICIPANTS: Preschoolers

INVITATIONS: Put "mirror" contact or wrapping paper inside invitation.
DECORATIONS: Mirrors
REFRESHMENTS: Hot dogs, Tater Tots
ACTIVITIES: Fingerplays

THEME: Mixed-up Daze
SCHEDULE: Summer night.
PARTICIPANTS: Third through sixth graders
INVITATIONS: Use mirror writing
DECORATIONS: Pictures hung upside down, anything that's not "usual" party decorations.
REFRESHMENTS: **Dump Punch,** Sloppy Joes
ACTIVITIES: Everybody's It, **Pancake Pandemonium, The Glob**

THEME: Mother/Daughter Chocolate
SCHEDULE: Winter Saturday AM
PARTICIPANTS: Mother/daughters of grades one through six
INVITATIONS: Hand out chocolate bars wrapped in invitations.
DECORATIONS: Arrange small groups of chairs in circles. Make it pretty! Ribbon streamers, flowers, pastel tablecloths
REFRESHMENTS: Hot chocolate, finger sandwiches
ACTIVITIES: Speaker, **Rubbed Memories**

THEME: Nature Expedition
SCHEDULE: Early summer or spring day
PARTICIPANTS: Any age, but don't make too big an age difference.
INVITATIONS: Enclose or use a leaf pattern
DECORATIONS: None needed
REFRESHMENTS: **Bumpy Peanutty Treats**
ACTIVITIES: **Nature Scavenger Hunt**

THEME: Night of Mysteries
SCHEDULE: Friday night
PARTICIPANTS: Older children

INVITATIONS: Write on construction paper, question mark, or in code.
DECORATIONS: Lots of question marks leading to party room
REFRESHMENTS: **Scripture Cake**
ACTIVITIES: Solve coded verses, mazes, and word searches

THEME: Tyke Hike
SCHEDULE: Summer day
PARTICIPANTS: Preschoolers and their families
INVITATIONS: Tie a shoestring around the invitation.
DECORATIONS: None needed
REFRESHMENTS: **Zipper Bag Pudding,** fruit and vegetable snacks
ACTIVITIES: Use the hike to raise money for missions.

THEME: No Girls Allowed—Boys Only!
SCHEDULE: Friday overnighter
PARTICIPANTS: Fifth- and sixth-grade boys and sponsors
INVITATIONS: Write "No Girls Allowed" with a red marker on front of invitation
DECORATIONS: Tents in a backyard
REFRESHMENTS: **Tooth Chippers,** dip and chips, sandwiches
ACTIVITIES: **Stinky Shoe Relay, The Glob**

THEME: No-Left-Turn Party
SCHEDULE: Some Saturday in spring
PARTICIPANTS: Second- through fourth-graders
INVITATIONS: Stop signs
DECORATIONS: Road signs
REFRESHMENTS: **Pretzel Perfections**

THEME: Not-Bored Games Tournament
SCHEDULE: Some nice evening—summer or winter
PARTICIPANTS: Families

INVITATIONS: Make invitations to resemble a checkerboard.
DECORATIONS: Set up game tables, float balloons.
REFRESHMENTS: Let each family bring favorite snacks to share.
ACTIVITIES: All kinds of games, **Ticktacktoe, Three Friends in a Row**

THEME: Out-of-This-World Space Party
SCHEDULE: Any time
PARTICIPANTS: Grades one through six
INVITATIONS: Spaceship
DECORATIONS: Rockets, spaceships, stars
REFRESHMENTS: **Salty Satellites,** Oreo orbit cookies
ACTIVITIES: **The Glob,** arrange a "Space Walk" obstacle course.

THEME: Painting Party
SCHEDULE: Cool summer morning
PARTICIPANTS: Preschoolers
INVITATIONS: Place paint splashes across invitations after printing.
DECORATIONS: Paint buckets, brushes, easels
REFRESHMENTS: Milk and graham crackers
ACTIVITIES: **Water Painting,** finger painting, easel painting

THEME: Paper Sack Party
SCHEDULE: Any fun day
PARTICIPANTS: Preschoolers/second graders
INVITATIONS: Printed on mini paper bags
DECORATIONS: All kinds of bags!
REFRESHMENTS: Bring a sack lunch
ACTIVITIES: Paper sack relay (unpack—put on—repack) make litter bags

THEME: Planting Party
SCHEDULE: Spring Saturday
PARTICIPANTS: Older preschoolers and teachers
INVITATIONS: Printed on package of flower seeds

DECORATIONS: Flowerpots, seed packets, potting plants
REFRESHMENTS: **Hole-in-One Sundaes**
ACTIVITIES: Plant seeds in the church flower beds; plant flowers for shut-ins.

THEME: Play Off-Pay Off
SCHEDULE: Otherwise boring day
PARTICIPANTS: All children
INVITATIONS: Printed on play money
DECORATIONS: Not necessary
REFRESHMENTS: Popcorn, cold drinks
ACTIVITIES: Play all kinds of games with sort of a round robin play-off.

THEME: Pig-Out Progressive Party
SCHEDULE: Friday night
PARTICIPANTS: Older children and adult sponsors
INVITATIONS: Pig-shaped
DECORATIONS: Not necessary
REFRESHMENTS: Progressive dinner, someone needs to serve **Oink-oink Corn Bread**

THEME: Preschoolers and Parents Picnic
SCHEDULE: Saturday: 11 AM to 1 PM
PARTICIPANTS: Preschoolers and parents
INVITATIONS: Place invitations in miniature picnic baskets or on that shape
DECORATIONS: Not needed
REFRESHMENTS: Potluck picnic fare
ACTIVITIES: Attention given to preschoolers having a good time

THEME: Promised Land Party
SCHEDULE: Flexible
PARTICIPANTS: Older children.
INVITATIONS: Write on a map of Israel
DECORATIONS: None
REFRESHMENTS: Whatever you choose, call it "manna!"
ACTIVITIES: Synagogue field trip

THEME: Tennis Shoes Tournament
SCHEDULE: Summer evening
PARTICIPANTS: Boys, grades one through six
INVITATIONS: Tennis shoe shape
DECORATIONS: None
REFRESHMENTS: Corn dogs, chips, brownies
ACTIVITIES: **Obstacle Course,** all kinds of relays

THEME: Reason for the Season Party
SCHEDULE: Date of any major holiday or one you have decided the world needs!
PARTICIPANTS: Children
INVITATIONS: In keeping with your "season"
DECORATIONS: In keeping with your "season"
REFRESHMENTS: **Dump Punch,** sandwiches, dip and chips
ACTIVITIES: The favorite games of the children involved

THEME: Sail with Paul Seminar
SCHEDULE: Friday 7 PM to Saturday, 8:30 AM
PARTICIPANTS: Older children
INVITATIONS: Silhouette of Paul or a sailboat.
DECORATIONS: Sailboat made from picnic table—use dowel rod and white sheet.
REFRESHMENTS: Tuna sandwiches, lots of snacks, individual boxed cereal for breakfast
ACTIVITIES: **Chariot Chases,** read a children's book about Paul, relays.

THEME: Say "Cheese" Party
SCHEDULE: Saturday afternoon
PARTICIPANTS: Fourth- through sixth-graders
INVITATIONS: Write on a wedge of cheese cut from gold or yellow paper.
DECORATIONS: Plastic mice, cheese, photographs of participants that they brought to the party
REFRESHMENTS: Toasted cheese sandwiches, cheese curls, cold drinks
ACTIVITIES: **Say Cheese, Camera Scavenger Hunt**

THEME: Sand, Water, and Mud Day

SCHEDULE: Morning
PARTICIPANTS: Preschoolers
INVITATIONS: Fold invitation and insert into a small seashell
DECORATIONS: None
REFRESHMENTS: **Mud Balls**
ACTIVITIES: **Mud Play**

THEME: Share-a-Lunch with the Bunch
SCHEDULE: Saturday noon
PARTICIPANTS: Children and their sponsors
INVITATIONS: On different colors of lunch sacks
DECORATIONS: None needed
REFRESHMENTS: See "Activities."
ACTIVITIES: Make sanwiches to share with homeless. Study the story of the good Samaritan.

THEME: Shepherd and Sheep
SCHEDULE: Summer morning
PARTICIPANTS: Preschool, fours, fives, and grades one through three.
INVITATIONS: Lambs made from cotton balls
DECORATIONS: Stuffed sheep, adults dressed in Bible costumes
REFRESHMENTS: Vanilla ice-cream "lamb." Cover ice cream with shredded coconut.
ACTIVITIES: Visit a farm. Read the book *A Certain Small Shepherd*.

THEME: Ship Ahoy
SCHEDULE: Saturday
PARTICIPANTS: First- through sixth-graders.
INVITATIONS: Sailboat shape with mini roll of Lifesavers enclosed.
DECORATIONS: Go to a park that has a lake or pond.
REFRESHMENTS: **High Seas Sandwiches**, fruit punch
ACTIVITIES: **Find Your Match, Mate; Kid Overboard**

THEME: Showing Off—Showing Art
SCHEDULE: Summer
PARTICIPANTS: Four-year-olds through sixth-graders
INVITATIONS: Paint cans, artist palette.
DECORATIONS: Easels, paint, crayons, brushes
REFRESHMENTS: **Confetti** or **Kaleidoscope Korn**
ACTIVITIES: Paint and draw pictures. Display pictures for all to enjoy. Everyone should receive a ribbon of some kind.

THEME: Shut-in Sing-a-Long
SCHEDULE: Sunday afternoon or a Saturday
PARTICIPANTS: Children and their sponsors
DECORATIONS: None needed
REFRESHMENTS: Take cookies, **Dump Punch**, peppermint candies, and little loaves of bread or crackers to shut-ins.
ACTIVITIES: Visit shut-ins and sing to or with them. Share your goodies.

THEME: Sink It, Swat It, Smack It Party
SCHEDULE: Summer evening
PARTICIPANTS: Grades one through six
INVITATIONS: Large golf ball shape
DECORATIONS: None
REFRESHMENTS: Snacks, cool drinks
ACTIVITIES: Go to play miniature golf

THEME: Soup and Sing
SCHEDULE: Winter evening
PARTICIPANTS: Friday night
INVITATIONS: Make a word search in a soup bowl picture.
DECORATIONS: None
REFRESHMENTS: Soup, crackers (Only put in things kids like to eat!)
ACTIVITIES: Sing fun songs, choruses hymns. Play "Name that Tune!"

THEME: Star Search
SCHEDULE: Any good night

PARTICIPANTS: Families
INVITATIONS: Giant star
DECORATIONS: Star garlands
REFRESHMENTS: Milky Way candy
ACTIVITIES: Star gazing with a telescope; no talent, talent show

THEME: Stuck on a Sticky Good Time
SCHEDULING: Snowy or rainy day
PARTICIPANTS: Older children, parents, or sponsors
INVITATIONS: Enclose a wrapped piece of taffy.
DECORATIONS: None necessary
REFRESHMENTS: **Tasty Taffy**
ACTIVITIES: Have a taffy pull, sing-along

THEME: Summer Sip and Slide
SCHEDULE: Summer day
PARTICIPANTS: Older preschoolers, first- through sixth-graders
INVITATIONS: Tape a drinking straw to the invitation. Remind children to wear swim clothes under playclothes.
DECORATIONS: None.
REFRESHMENTS: **Summer Breeze Cooler**
ACTIVITIES: **Slide-Away**

THEME: Sundae Sunday
SCHEDULE: After church Sunday evening.
PARTICIPANTS: All children and parents.
INVITATIONS: Write invitation on ice-cream shape or sundae shape or wooden ice-cream spoons.
DECORATIONS: Not needed
REFRESHMENTS: Vanilla ice cream and several toppings
ACTIVITIES: Banana Relay, chorus singing, devotions

THEME: Tacky Party
SCHEDULE: On a winter evening
PARTICIPANTS: All children, preschoolers, parents

INVITATIONS: Printed on a paper "tacky" shirt
DECORATIONS: Set tables with newspapers for cloths, eat off foil pans, plastic forks, anything "tacky."
REFRESHMENTS: Something warm—chili, soup, hot dogs
ACTIVITIES: **You Look Ridiculous Relay.** Have a contest to see who came dressed the "tackiest!"

THEME: Tacos and Tunes
SCHEDULING: Fall
PARTICIPANTS: Children's choirs and their sponsors
INVITATIONS: Musical note wearing a sombrero
DECORATIONS: Mexican hats, pinatas
REFRESHMENTS: Tacos and all the trimmings!
ACTIVITIES: Make tacos; eat tacos; practice for a musical.

THEME: Tater Time
SCHEDULE: November
PARTICIPANTS: Families
INVITATIONS: Tater shaped
DECORATIONS: Baskets, bags of potatoes
REFRESHMENTS: Tater Tots or top your own baked potato
ACTIVITIES: Play "Hot Potato," have potato relays.

THEME: Thanksgiving Open House
SCHEDULE: Sunday before Thanksgiving
PARTICIPANTS: Families
INVITATIONS: On turkey shapes
DECORATIONS: "Turkeys," pumpkins, gourds, Indian corn
REFRESHMENTS: **Cinnamony Biscuits, Orange Delight Toast,** orange juice and milk
ACTIVITIES: Have an "I am thankful . . ." time. Sing "thankful songs."

THEME: Tree Tea
SCHEDULING: Early summer.
PARTICIPANTS: Mother/daughter

INVITATIONS: Printed on a tree shape, enclose a tea bag
DECORATIONS: Need a big tree and a picnic table or two
REFRESHMENTS: Dainty finger sandwiches, cookies, tea
ACTIVITIES: Relaxed conversation, no games

THEME: T-Shirt Affair
SCHEDULE: Summer day
PARTICIPANTS: Older children
INVITATIONS: T-shirt shape
DECORATIONS: Hang T-shirts around room. Ask participants to wear their favorite T-shirts.
REFRESHMENTS: Cake in T-Shirt shape, cold drinks
ACTIVITIES: **One-of-a-Kind T-shirt**

THEME: Twinsy Party
SCHEDULE: Halloween
PARTICIPANTS: First through third graders
INVITATIONS: Joined paper dolls
DECORATIONS: Two of every decoration
REFRESHMENTS: Double burgers, Twinkies, Doublemint gum
ACTIVITIES: Encourage attenders to bring a friend and dress as twins. Have a "parade." Play games where teams of two play.

THEME: Up, Up, and Away
SCHEDULE: Spring holiday
PARTICIPANTS: Grades one through six
INVITATIONS: Write invitations on inflated balloons, deflate and mail.
DECORATIONS: Parachutes, "Hot air balloons" made from helium-filled balloons
REFRESHMENTS: Cotton candy, pink lemonade
ACTIVITIES: **Balloon Ballyball**

THEME: Wanted Alive Jamboree
SCHEDULE: Sunday morning
PARTICIPANTS: Older children and parents, Children wake up prospects and bring them to church for breakfast and Sunday School.
INVITATIONS: Wanted posters
DECORATIONS: None
REFRESHMENTS: **Wake-Up-Wrap-Ups,** cold milk
ACTIVITIES: Fellowship talk at breakfast, introduce to rest of group, go to Sunday School

THEME: Western Roundup
SCHEDULE: Fall
PARTICIPANTS: All children
INVITATIONS: Boots, rope, bandanas
DECORATIONS: Sawhorse with saddle, bales of hay, cowboy hats
REFRESHMENTS: Sloppy Joes, baked beans, cobbler.
ACTIVITIES: "Calf roping" (tossing a rope at a turned upside-down chair leg) Play **The Glob** but call it "Roundup."

THEME: Winter Indoor Picnic
SCHEDULE: Cold, winter day
PARTICIPANTS: Families or a Sunday School department
INVITATIONS: Written on a mitten
DECORATIONS: Snow scenes on windows; have a fire in a fireplace, if possible.
REFRESHMENTS: **Chewy Snowballs,** picnic fare
ACTIVITIES: Play kickball if you are in a gym, or indoor baseball played with a soft ball.

THEME: Wonderful Works Affair
SCHEDULE: Saturday morning
PARTICIPANTS: Families
INVITATIONS: Use church bulletin, newsletter, and posters to invite families to participate.
DECORATIONS: Splatter paper tablecloths with paint. Dry before using to display crafts.
REFRESHMENTS: **Crunchies**
ACTIVITIES: Invite church members to display handmade crafts. Lead in carnival games.

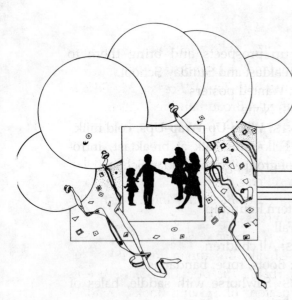

12
"Any Other Suggestions?"

Good Resources to Help You

Books of Games and Activities

Baratta-Lorton, Mary. *Workjobs*. Menlo Park, California: Addison-Wesley Publishing Company, 1972.

Bolton, Barbara J. *How to Do Bible Learning Activities, Grades 1-6, Book 1*. Ventura, California: International Center for Learning, 1982.

Brandreth, Gyles. *The World's Best Indoor Games*. New York: Pantheon Books, 1982.

Branson, Mary Kinney. *A Carousel of Countries*. Birmingham: New Hope.

Crabtree, June. *Learning Center Ideas for Ages 3 Through 14*. Cincinnati: Standard Publishing, 1977.

Farnette, Cherrie, et al. *At Least a Thousand Things to Do, a Career-Awareness Activity Book*. Nashville: Incentive Publications, 1977.

Fiarotta, Phyllis and Noel Fiarotta. *Be What You Want to Be! The Complete Dress-Up and Pretend Craft Book*. New York: Workman Publishing Company, 1977.

Fluegelman, Andrew, ed. *The New Games Book, Play Hard, Play Fair, Nobody Hurt*. Garden City, N.Y.: A Headlands Press Book, Dolphin Books, Doubleday & Company, Inc., 1976.

Forte, Imogene, et al. *Pumpkins, Pinwheels and Peppermint Packages, Second Edition*. Nashville: Incentive Publications, 1974.

———. *Puddles and Wings and Grapevine Swings, Things to Make and do with Nature's Treasures*. Nashville: Incentive Publications, 1982.

Frank, Marjorie. *I Can Make a Rainbow*. (Nashville, Incentive Publications, 1976.)

Gaither, Gloria and Shirley Dobson. *Let's Make a Memory*. Waco, Texas, Word Book Publishers, 1983.

Hohmann, Mary, et al. *Young Children in Action, A Manual for Preschool Educators*. Ypsilanti, Mich.: The High/Scope Press, 1979.

Koch, Kenneth. *Wishes, Lies, and Dreams, Teaching Children to Write Poetry*. New York: Perennial Library, Harper & Row Publishers, 1978.

Le Fever, Marlene D. *Creative Teaching Methods, Be an Effective Christian Educator*. Elgin, Ill.: David C. Cook Publishing, Co. 1985.

Long, Lynette. *On My Own*. Washington, D.C.: Acropolis Books Ltd., 1984.

MacKenzie, Joy. *The Big Book of Bible Crafts and Projects*. Grand Rapids, Mich.: The Zondervan Corporation, 1982.

Rice, Wayne and Mike Yaconelli. *Play It!* Grand Rapids, Mich.: Youth Specialties, Zondervan Publishing House, 1986.

Rohnke, Karl. *Silver Bullets*. Hamilton, Mass.: Project Adventure, Inc., 1984.

Rowen, Dolores. *Easy to Make Crafts for Preteens and Youth*. Glendale, Calif.: G/L Publications, 1976.

Smith, Frank Hart. *Reaching People Through Recreation*. Nashville: Convention Press, 1973.

Sobel, Jeffrey. *Everybody Wins*. New York: Walker Publishing Company, Inc., 1983.

Sullivan, Molly. *Feeling Strong, Feeling Free: Movement Exploration for Young Children*. Washington, D.C.: National Association for the Education of Young Children, 1982.

Swadley, Elizabeth. *Christmas at Home*. Nashville: Broadman Press, 1975.

Williams, Nancy S. *Inside and Occupied, Over 500 Ideas for Parents Whose Children "Have Nothing to Do!"* Scottsdale, Penn.: Herald Press, 1982.

Wilt, Joy and Bill Watson. *Relationship Builders, 156 Activities and Games for Building Relationships, Ages 8-12*. Waco, Tex.: Word Educational Products Division, 1978.

Wolfe, Marcia. *Easy Crafts for Children*. Cincinnati: Standard Publishing, 1985.

Books of Stories and Poems for Children

Baw, Cindy and Paul C. Brownlow. *Children of the Bible*. Fort Worth: Brownlow Publishing Company, Inc., 1984.

Caudill, Rebecca. *A Certain Small Shepherd*. New York: Holt, Rinehart and Winston, 1965.

Coleman, William L. *Before You Tuck Me In*. Minneapolis: Bethany House Publishers, 1985.

———. *The Courageous Christians*. Elgin, Ill.: Chariot Books, 1982.

———. *If Animals Could Talk*. Minneapolis: Bethany House Publishers, 1987.

Doney, Meryl. *How Our Bible Came to Us, The Story of the Book that Changed the World*. Tring, England: A Lion Book, 1985.

———. *Jesus, The Man Who Changed History*. Tring, England: A Lion Book, 1988.

Heath, Lou and Beth Taylor, *Reading My Bible in Fall*. Nashville: Broadman Press, 1986.

———. *Reading My Bible in Spring*. Nashville: Broadman Press, 1986.

———. *Reading My Bible in Summer*. Nashville: Broadman Press, 1986.

———. *Reading My Bible in Winter*. Nashville: Broadman Press, 1986.

Linam, Gail. *God's People, A Book of Children's Sermons*. Nashville: Broadman Press, 1986.

Robinson, Barbara. *The Best Christmas Pageant Ever*. Wheaton, Ill.: Living Books, Tyndale House Publishing, 1972.)

Silverstein, Shel. *A Light in the Attic*. New York: Harper & Row, Publishers, 1981.

———. *Where the Sidewalk Ends*. New York: Harper and Row, 1974.

Books About Childhood Development and Guiding Behavior

Allen, Dr. Roger and Ron Rose. *Common Sense Discipline*. Fort Worth, Tex.: Sweet Publishing, 1986.

Berne, Patricia H. and Louis M. Savary. *Building Self-Esteem in Children*. New York: Continuum Publishing Co., 1981.

Brazelton, Terry, M.D. *To Listen to a Child*. Reading, Mass.: Addison-Wesley, 1984.

Cherry, Clare. *Creative Play for the Developing Child*. Belmont, Calif.: Fearon Pitman Publishers, Inc., 1976.

———. *Think of Something Quiet*. Belmont, Calif.: Fearon Pitman Publishers, 1983.

Collins, W. Andrew, ed. *Development During Middle Childhood (The Years from Six to Twelve)*. Washington, D.C.: National Academy Press, 1984.

Hart, Leslie A. *Human Brain and Human Learning*. New York: Longman, Inc., 1983.

Lall, Getta R., Ph.D. and Bernard M. Lall, Ph.D.

Ways Children Learn. Springfield, Ill.: Charles C. Thomas, Publishers, 1983.

Price, B. Max. *Understanding Today's Children*. Nashville: Convention Press, 1982.

Saunders, Antoinette, Ph.D. and Bonnie Rensberg. *The Stress-Proof Child*. New York: Holt, Rinehart, and Winston, 1984.

Waldrop, C. Sybil. *Understanding Today's Preschoolers*. Nashville: Convention Press, 1982.

Williams, Linda Verlee. *Teaching for the Two-Sided Mind*. Englewood Cliffs, N.J.: Prentice-Hall, Inc. 1983.

Books of Music for Preschoolers and Children

Blankenship, Mark. *DiscipleYouth Songs* Nashville: Broadman Press, 1984.

———. *Songs for Fellowship and Recreation, Singing Is Fun!* Nashville: Broadman Press, 1978.

Glazer, Tom, *Eye Winker Tom Tinker Chin Chopper, a Collection of Musical Fingerplays*. Garden City, N.Y.: Doubleday & Company, Inc., 1973.

Hunter, Ilene and Marilyn Judson. *Simple Folk Instruments to Make and Play*. New York: A Fireside Book, Published by Simon and Schuster, 1977.

Jones, Nettie Lou and Saxe Adams, comps. and eds. *Songs for Children*. Nashville: Broadman Press, 1964.

Jones, Nettie Lou and William J. Reynolds, eds. *Songs for 4's and 5's*. Nashville: Broadman Press, 1960.

Kirkland, Terry and Richard Ham. *Pocket Book of Fun Songs*. Nashville: Broadman Press, 1974.

Leach, Bill F. and Paul Bobbitt, comps. and eds. *Junior Hymnal*. Nashville: Broadman Press, 1964.

Leach, Bill F., Talmadge Butler, Saxe Adams. *Songs for the Young Child*. Nashville: Broadman Press, 1971.

Rhea, Claude and Carolyn. *A Child's Life in Song*. Nashville: Broadman Press, 1964.

Books of Refreshments and Snacks

Bershad, Carol and Deborah Bernick. *Bodyworks. The Kids Guide to Food and Physical Fitness*. New York: Random House, 1979.

Boteler, Alison. *The Children's Party Handbook, Fantasy, Food, and Fun*. New York: Barron's Educational Series, Inc., 1986.

Haas, Carolyn Buhai. *The Book of Recipes for Fun, Creative Learning Activities for Home and School*. Northfield, Ill.: CBH Publishing, Inc., 1980.

Loo, Miriam B. *Meals of Many Lands, A Cookbook for Children*. Colorado Springs: Current Inc., 1980.

———. *Special Dishes for Special Days*. Colorado Springs: Current Inc., 1980.

———. *Holiday Cookbook for Boys and Girls*. Watermill Press, 1981.

———. *Young Children's Mix and Fix Cookbook*. New York: *Parents'* Magazine Enterprises, Inc., 1975.

Indexes

Games and Activities

Ideas, Plans, and Themes

Refreshments